ONLY THE GOOD DIE YOUNG

ROBERT JOHNSON, BRIAN JONES & AMY WINEHOUSE: THE ROLLERCOASTER RIDE OF ROCK'N'ROLL TRAGEDY

Publisher and Creative Director: Nick Wells
Project Editor and Picture Research: Sara Robson
Art Director: Mike Spender
Layout Design: Jane Ashley
Digital Design and Production: Chris Herbert

Special thanks to: Laura Bulbeck, Helen Crust, Alex Davidson, Anna Groves, Geoffrey Meadon, Polly Prior and Catherine Taylor

First published 2012 by
FLAME TREE PUBLISHING
Crabtree Hall, Crabtree Lane
Fulham, London SW6 6TY
United Kingdom

www.flametreepublishing.com

Music information site: www.flametreemusic.com

12 14 16 15 13

1 3 5 7 9 10 8 6 4 2

The CIP record for this book is available from the British Library.

ISBN: 978-0-85775-394-6

Printed in Singapore

ONLY THE GOOD DIE YOUNG

ROBERT JOHNSON, BRIAN JONES & AMY WINEHOUSE: THE ROLLERCOASTER RIDE OF ROCK'N'ROLL TRAGEDY

JASON DRAPER AND JIM DRISCOLL
FOREWORD BY JOEL McIVER

FLAME TREE
PUBLISHING

CONTENTS

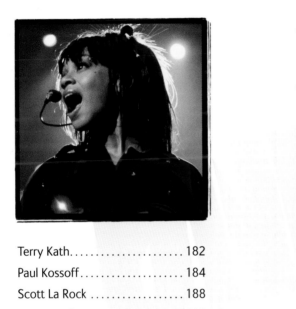

FOREWORD

The ultimate party-pooper, Death, comes to us all in the end, damn him and his stupid rusty scythe. Your eventual meeting with him is one of the simplest, and also most irritating, facts of life – and one especially irksome for any creative musician, whose innermost urge is to get songs composed, performed and recorded (preferably while making a living at the same time) before the Grim Reaper comes calling.

It's a sad fact that professional musicians, whose lifestyles take them closer and more frequently to the edge of the abyss than other, less driven folks, tend to die younger than most of the population. This excellent collection demonstrates

this point so well that by the time you get to the end of the book, you'll find it hard to believe that anyone who picks up a guitar or microphone will see the other side of 30.

Only The Good Die Young is no mere anthology of obituaries, however. This book is nothing less than a celebration of the life and work of 111 musicians whose appointment with Death came early, but who still managed to change people's lives on a permanent basis before that end point. How many of us can make a similar claim? And yet that's what we all yearn for: the ability to leave an imperishable legacy after we're gone.

Like life itself, this book is bittersweet. It's saddening beyond belief to read what happened to all these young talents, often in circumstances that could easily have been avoided. Did Amy Winehouse really need that second bottle of vodka? Did Randy Rhoads really have to climb into that plane? Couldn't Jeff Buckley have left that dip in the river until another day? Then there are the musicians whose lives were taken by other people, like Tupac Shakur and Jaco Pastorius – and even Brian Jones and Jimi Hendrix, if you believe the conspiracy theories. So much hatred. So much bloodshed....

Of course, drugs and booze played their devilish part. Tour hard, play hard, grip it, chug it and shoot it: this was the exit method for Tommy Bolin, John Bonham, Steve Clark, Keith Moon, Charlie Parker, Jimmy 'The Rev' Sullivan, Bon Scott, Hillel Slovak and Layne Staley among many, many others. But at least they were having fun, for the most part: the saddest tales of all, for me at least, focus on the artists who, sick of this mortal coil, ended it all themselves. The grim roll-call includes Kurt Cobain, most infamously, as well as Ian Curtis and Nick Drake (perhaps inadvertently in his case? We'll never know).

Not that every story has a simple reason behind it, though. Life, or rather death, is like that. What really happened to Jim Morrison, dead in a Paris bathtub? And Richey Edwards, declared dead after seven years but still, in theory at least,

perfectly capable of walking into a Welsh pub tomorrow? Then there's Sid Vicious, who died at the hands of a syringe full of heroin but who may, or may not, have murdered his girlfriend before shooting up one last time. These are the people who fascinate us most, because we don't know what their last actions, their final thoughts or their ultimate conclusions were before they 'drew their terminal breath' (thanks, Eric Idle).

AIDS. Anorexia. Heart conditions. Bullets. Fists. Polydrug intoxication. Revenge. All these are here in some form or shape, and it's almost never good news when any of them encounter a human being. But this is no collection of ghoulishness: *Only The Good Die Young* isn't about death, it's about life, and what happens while people are living. Paradoxically, when it comes to music there is a strong argument in favour of impending mortality: faced with a permanently ticking clock in reverse, an impenetrable black wall silently drawing closer every day, the awareness that one day in the not-too-distant future their family and friends will be sipping sherry and eating Hula-Hoops at their funeral, many musicians feel driven to create their best work while they still can.

Name an artist whose best work came in his or her later life. Go on, just one. There are a few: Seasick Steve, perhaps, or Johnny Cash. But these are few and far between. In general, music is an expression of youthful vitality as much as it is a cerebral or intellectual aesthetic. Life is music. That is the message of *Only The Good Die Young*, and because this book hammers home that message repeatedly, by its end you may find yourself inspired to write a song yourself. After all, isn't that the point?

Joel McIver

INTRODUCTION

'It's better to burn out than to fade away.' So sang Neil Young – 66 and releasing his 34th studio album, *Americana*, at the time of writing – in his 1979 song 'Hey Hey, My My (Into The Black)'. 'I hope I die before I get old' was Pete Townshend's wish in The Who's 1965 single 'My Generation', last played live on stage in Perth, on 4 April 2009. Aged 63 then, and now eligible for a bus pass, Townshend is one of only two of The Who's surviving original band members, along with frontman Roger Daltrey.

Yet why this obsession with an early death? If you're holding this book, you may be able to answer that yourself. After all, a title such as *Only The Good Die Young* hardly resonates with affirmations of life. Something must have drawn you to it. Adolescents – even young adults in their early-to-mid 20s, as many of the entrants in this book

were – often seem to be preoccupied with mortality. Young enough that death should be a far-off event, the likes of Ian Curtis and Jim Morrison pored over its mysteries, revealing their obsessions in lyrics to songs such as Joy Division's 'Atrocity Exhibition' or The Doors' bluntly titled 'The End'. The former singer hanged himself at 23, having received comparisons to the latter, who had died in a bath at 27.

And therein lies another mystery. This book will introduce you to something dubbed the '27 Club' – though membership comes at a price. A bewildering number of icons – Kurt Cobain, Jimi Hendrix, Janis Joplin and Amy Winehouse among them – have died, with eerie coincidence, aged 27. Almost a quarter of the 111 artists in this book joined the 'club' – including blues musician Robert Johnson, our earliest-dated entrant. The third member of the club that opened in 1892, Johnson also has one of the most enigmatic biographies here, taking in deals with the Devil, revolutionary music and death by poison.

Unsurprisingly, all manner of other ingested drugs pervade the book too, with heroin, either directly or indirectly, contributing to an alarming number of deaths. Yet, while one extreme sees Los Angeles' hardcore punk Darby Crash intentionally buying enough smack to commit suicide, a large majority of drug users overdose by accident. It's well known that Nick Drake was clinically depressed, but it's also impossible to say whether he took his own life or was hoping that enough antidepressants would offer momentary respite from the pain of living. He's certainly not the only artist for whom even legally prescribed drugs proved fatal.

After years of heavy heroin abuse, pioneering bebop saxophonist Charlie Parker's body simply gave out while he sat watching television. The coroner who autopsied the musician placed Parker's age somewhere in his 50s; he was 34. 'Death by misadventure' goes hand-in-hand with sensual derangement: by the time she died, Amy Winehouse's liver was more pickled than the onions on sale in her local pub; Brian Jones sank like a Rolling Stone when he took to his swimming pool after a party. But plenty of stone-cold sober accidents also prove fatal. In fact, of all the fatalities not related to drugs, plane crashes just about outweigh suicide, with the deaths of Buddy Holly, The Big Bopper and Ritchie Valens (the youngest musician in the book, aged just 17 when he died) in one fatal collision being considered the day the music died'.

Meanwhile, you've got to be truly unlucky to not only die in a bus crash, but also fly through the window then have the bus topple over and land on top of you: a fate that befell Metallica bassist Cliff Burton. If that example seems bizarre, some deaths are just inexplicable. Bobby Fuller was found in a car, covered in petrol but not burned. His death has been variously attributed to suicide (through inhaling petrol fumes), 'accidental asphyxiation' and even murder by notorious 1960s serial killer Charles Manson. Manic Street Preachers' lyricist and guitarist Richey Edwards disappeared off the face of the earth in 1995. Though officially pronounced dead in 2008, the lack of conclusive evidence still leaves the door open for doubt to creep in.

Tragically, deaths from natural causes are in relatively short supply in these pages. Karen Carpenter's heart failed when she was just 32. Years of anorexia had put strains on a body that might otherwise have been hale and hearty for years to come. Legendary jazz bassist and Joni Mitchell sideman Jaco Pastorius died of a brain haemorrhage after slipping into a coma – but then brawling with a bouncer just days before wouldn't have done him any good. Eazy-E's output is obsessed with violence, yet ironically he was one of the very few artists in this book to have died from natural causes, succumbing to AIDS just weeks after diagnosis.

Speaking of Karen Carpenter – who rose to fame as one half of the brother-and-sister duo The Carpenters – family affairs add another layer of tragedy. As a solo artist, Andy Gibb enjoyed mainstream successes and even a brief chart battle with his siblings The Bee Gees. The four brothers worked closely together in the studio, creating hits such as the chart-topping 'Shadow Dancing' in 1978. The youngest of the brothers, Andy died just five days after his 30th birthday. In 1997, alt-rock hero Jeff Buckley died, also aged 30, after being dragged into the slipstream of a passing tugboat while swimming in Memphis's Wolf River Harbour. Buckley lived a mere two years longer than his father, Tim; the pair had met only once before Buckley senior died of an accidental heroin overdose in 1975.

'It's better to burn out than to fade away.' So wrote Kurt Cobain in his suicide note – but then he was a heroin addict who wanted to call his last album *I Hate Myself And Want To Die*. 'Obviously his interpretation should not be taken

to mean there's only two ways to go and one of them is death,' Neil Young told the *NME* in 1995, but Cobain's actions chilled Young to the bone. He would write his 1994 album, *Sleeps With Angels*, in Cobain's memory, going on to be crowned 'The Godfather Of Grunge' and recording another album, *Mirror Ball*, with Nirvana's Seattle grunge contemporaries Pearl Jam. Yet none of these reactions could ever reverse Cobain's action: a young man had taken his own life and, like every artist in this book, left a closing chapter that sometimes threatens to overshadow the artistic achievements most of us would wish to focus on.

Look outside: there's a life to be lived, and many of the artists in this book lived it to the full. Many others, however, barely reached their full potential. Having revolutionized country music for women in the industry, Patsy Cline died just as her career was taking off; rising star Jeff Buckley never finished recordings for his second album; Charles Haddon, of Ou Est Le Swimming Pool, did not even live long enough to see his band's first album released. So while this book tells of many deaths, it also celebrates life. We are lucky that Marc Bolan invented glam rock. Or that Otis Redding had just enough time to record '(Sittin' On) The Dock Of The Bay'; Gram Parsons rescued country music

from obscurity; Amy Winehouse introduced a new generation to soul music; and Jimi Hendrix revolutionized the electric guitar. We are lucky for every moment we have.

So is it better to burn out? John Lennon's opinion – expressed just three months before he was shot dead in December 1980, at the age of 40 – was that, 'It's better to fade away like an old soldier than to burn out.... I worship the people who survive.' Perhaps 'survive' is the key word: life is difficult, but the memories we cherish, the friends and family we adore and, yes, the music we listen to, all this can only be enjoyed through life. The good die young? Tragically, this has often been the case, but the bigger tragedy is that these musical legends missed out on life, and might have been yet greater had they lived longer.

Jason Draper

GOOD YOUNG

A-Z OF ARTISTS

AALIYAH

ONE IN A MILLION

With a singer for a mother and entertainment lawyer for a father, Aaliyah Haughton seemed destined for fame. Perhaps the only thing more surprising than her debut album coming out at the age of 15 was the fact that the singer had already signed a distribution deal with Jive two years previously, and had performed live on stage with soul legend Gladys Knight at the age of 11.

Preceded by her R&B chart-topping debut single, 'Back And Forth', *Age Ain't Nothing But A Number* came out in 1994, reaching No. 3 in the US R&B charts and No. 18 in *Billboard*'s Top 200. Co-written and produced by R. Kelly – then himself riding high on the success of his *12 Play* album – Aaliyah's debut merged her delicate, high-pitched vocals with a harder, contemporary R&B sound. It subsequently emerged that Aaliyah and her mentor had married secretly – and illegally, as she was still a minor – on 31 August 1994. The singer's parents had the marriage annulled in January the following year.

HOT LIKE FIRE

Having established herself as one of the hottest new R&B stars of the 1990s, Aaliyah teamed up with the dream hip-hop production and songwriting duo of Timbaland and Missy Elliott for 1996's *One In A Million*. With the backing of major label Atlantic – one of the classic soul imprints of the 1960s – the album was an incredible success. For Timbaland and Missy Elliott, it was a step towards the era-defining hip-hop they would create in the late 1990s and early 2000s. For Aaliyah, it built upon her early promise, peaking at No. 2 in the R&B charts, while yielding six single releases, including the chart-topping title track.

ONLY THE
GOOD DIE YOUNG

Within a year, *One In A Million* would go double-platinum, by which point Aaliyah was making inroads into Hollywood. A graduate of the Detroit High School of the Performing Arts in 1997, she would contribute a song to that year's animated movie *Anastasia*, followed by another on the 1998 *Dr Doolittle* soundtrack, all in the run-up to executive-producing and contributing to the soundtrack for – and starring in – 2000's *Romeo Must Die*.

MiSS YOU

Such a work rate caused delays in the recording of Aaliyah's third album. Self-titled and released in July 2001, it topped the US album charts, replicated its predecessor's success and became her highest-charting album in the UK, peaking at No. 5. The following month, Aaliyah was in the Bahamas recording a promo video for the album's second single, 'Rock The Boat'. After filming finished ahead of schedule, the singer decided to return home. At the hands of an inexperienced pilot, the small plane – weighed down with filming equipment and an entourage including record label representatives, a personal stylist and production crew – crashed almost immediately after taking off, killing everyone on board. A wrongful death lawsuit filed against the Bahamas-based Blackhawk International Airways was settled out of court. Posthumous releases have kept the singer in the public eye throughout the following decade, while she continues to be credited with altering the landscape of 1990s R&B.

DATE OF BIRTH

16 January 1979

DATE OF DEATH

25 August 2001

GENRES

R&B, pop

JOHNNY ACE

ACE OF CLUBS

An early R&B star born in 'the birthplace of rock'n'roll' – Memphis, Tennessee – John Marshall Alexander, Jr cut his teeth as a pianist playing the Beale Street clubs as part of blues guitarist B.B. King's band in the late 1940s. When the bandleader left to pursue a recording career in Los Angeles, Alexander took over the group, renaming them The Beale Streeters and promoting himself to singer. In 1952, he signed to the Memphis–based Duke imprint, releasing his debut single, 'My Song', under the name Johnny Ace.

Enjoying a string of hits for Duke, Ace set out on the Chitlin' Circuit for most of 1954, playing the City Auditorium in Houston, Texas, on Christmas Day. During a break between sets, the singer was found backstage, playing with a gun and under the influence of alcohol. Accounts differ – some say he was playing Russian roulette, others, such as R&B singer Big Mama Thornton, that he was waving the weapon around. But what's indisputable is that the gun went off while Johnny Ace had it pointed to his head, killing him instantly.

DATE OF BIRTH

9 June 1929

DATE OF DEATH

25 December 1954

GENRES

R&B

ONLY THE
GOOD DIE YOUNG

CHRIS ACLAND

THE SCARS STILL SHOW

Drummer for the shoegazing band Lush, Chris Acland was one of the group's founding members alongside singer Merial Barham, guitarists Emma Anderson and Miki Berenyi, and bassist Steve Rippon. They signed to 4AD – home of pioneering soundscape artists Cocteau Twins – for their debut EP, 1989's *Scar*. Critical acclaim and a string of singles and EPs followed (including the 1990 *Mad Love* EP, produced by the Cocteaus' Robin Guthrie), while the band built a following, embarking on overseas tours with fellow shoegazers Ride.

By the time of 1992's *Spooky*, critical fervour had waned, though Lush maintained a fan base strong enough to release two more LPs. 1994's *Split* saw them become the first group to release two singles on the same day ('Hypocrite' and 'Desire Lines', 30 May 1994), though both were overshadowed by the emerging Britpop scene and failed to make the Top 40. 1996's *Lovelife* LP fared better, becoming their biggest–selling LP, reaching No. 8. Yet, despite finding a more upbeat sound, darker things were happening behind the scenes. After a US tour, Acland succumbed to growing depression and committed suicide by hanging himself in his parents' home.

DATE OF BIRTH

7 September 1966

DATE OF DEATH

17 October 1996

GENRES

Shoegazing, Britpop

ONLY THE
GOOD DIE YOUNG

DAVE ALEXANDER

PROTO-PUNK HELLRAISER

A founding member of Michigan proto-punks The Stooges, Dave Alexander (pictured second from the right) showed early signs of a wild streak. He met up with brothers Ron and Scott Asheton – future Stooges guitarist and drummer respectively – at Ann Arbor's Pioneer High School, later dropping out 45 minutes into the first day of his senior year, in 1965, in order to win a bet.

Together with legendary hellraiser Iggy Pop, the boys formed The Stooges, with Iggy as vocalist and Alexander as bassist. Despite being signed to Elektra for their 1968 self-titled debut LP, their uncompromisingly raw, heavy guitar sound and Iggy's confrontational presence kept commercial success at arm's length. A second, heavier album followed in 1970. Its title, *Fun House*, mirrored the freewheeling, carnivalesque behemoth the group had become. Yet Alexander's alcohol intake was too great even for the chemically infused troupe, and he was sacked from the band after being too drunk to play at Michigan's Goose Lake International Music Festival in 1970. Alexander's career never recovered and he died of a pulmonary oedema five years later – after being admitted to hospital for alcohol-related pancreatitis – aged just 27.

DATE OF BIRTH

3 June 1947

DATE OF DEATH

10 February 1975

GENRES

Proto-punk

DUANE ALLMAN

PEACHY KEEN

Perennially appearing at the top of any 'best guitarist' run-downs, in the five years that he spent as a recording musician Nashville-born Duane Allman appeared on over 25 studio LPs, while live albums bearing his name also stretch into double figures. Famed for being one half of The Allman Brothers, co-founded with brother Gregg, Duane appeared on recordings by artists as diverse as Wilson Pickett, Laura Nyro, Aretha Franklin, Boz Scaggs, Ronnie Hawkins, Eric Clapton and Lulu.

Allman and his younger brother learned guitar together – perhaps a welcome distraction for the boys, whose father was murdered when they were very young. After seeing B.B. King in concert, an obsession with the blues was born. Playing with a string of local acts from as early as 1961, the brothers formed their own groups, The Allman Joys and The Hour Glass, in 1965 and 1967 respectively. While The Hour Glass's self-titled debut – and its 1968 follow-up, *Power Of Love* – were relative disappointments for the brothers, it gave Duane all-important studio experience. He was soon picked up for session work at the legendary Fame Studios in Muscle Shoals, Alabama, where he made the bulk of his recordings.

OTHER ASSORTED SONGS

Duane formed The Allman Brothers in Florida with brother Gregg and a group of musicians that he'd taken to playing with. Honing their skills as a unit through endless jamming, the group's 1969 self-titled debut and 1970 follow-up, *Idlewild South*, were critical if not entirely commercial successes, paving the way for two of Duane's greatest achievements.

ONLY THE
GOOD DIE YOUNG

While in Miami recording 1971's *Layla And Other Assorted Love Songs* LP with Derek & The Dominos, Eric Clapton attended an Allman Brothers concert. Immediately stunned by the guitarist's performance, he asked Duane to join the Dominos' sessions – conceived as the laid-back alternative to the British guitarist's famed work with high-profile supergroups Cream and Blind Faith. Allman would lend his distinctive style to one of Clapton's most enduring songs, 'Layla'. Yet the brothers weren't just wowing their musician friends; in July 1971 they released their own breakthrough album, *Live At Fillmore East*, a live double-LP that peaked at No. 13 in the charts.

AIN'T WASTIN' TIME NO MORE

With interest in the Allmans at an all-time high, 10 years after the two brothers started playing together, they recorded their defining studio album. Including material recorded – but not used – for *Live At Fillmore East* (including the 33-minute 'Mountain Jam'), the double-album *Eat A Peach* also boasted Allman studio classics such as opener 'Ain't Waitin' Time No More', 'Blue Sky' and 'Little Martha'. It was hailed as a masterpiece, reaching No. 4 in the charts, though Duane would not see any of the acclaim. During a break from the late-1971 sessions for the album, while riding his motorcycle, Duane collided with a truck at high speed and died in hospital from internal injuries. There have been enough posthumously released live Allman Brothers albums to rival those issued during his lifetime, while The Allman Brothers Band has continued to play throughout the decades, earning a Lifetime Achievement Award at the 2012 Grammys.

DATE OF BIRTH

20 November 1946

DATE OF DEATH

29 October 1971

GENRES

Southern rock

ONLY THE
GOOD DIE YOUNG

MEL APPLEBY

TWO-HIT WONDER

Born in east London to British and Jamaican parents, Melanie Appleby (pictured on the right) made initial forays into modelling before recording two solo demo tracks in 1985 under the aegis of manager Alan Whitehead – a pioneer of London's table-dancing clubs. Asked if she had a partner she could sing with, Mel teamed up with her sister Kim in order to record a collection of demos as Mel & Kim.

The recordings caught the ear of Supreme label head honcho Nick East, who teamed the duo with legendary 1980s songwriting and production trio Stock Aitken Waterman. The result was 'Showing Out (Get Fresh At The Weekend)', a zeitgeist-capturing pop-club crossover hit built upon a naggingly infectious keyboard line and chorus refrain that took the single to No. 3 in the UK charts in 1986. Its follow-up, 'Respectable', hit the top spot the following year. Momentum stalled, however, after Mel was diagnosed with secondary cancer of the spine. Mel's immune system deteriorated as a result of the chemotherapy and she died of pneumonia in January 1990.

DATE OF BIRTH

11 July 1966

DATE OF DEATH

18 January 1990

GENRES

Pop

ONLY THE
GOOD DIE YOUNG

CHRIS BELL

WRITTEN IN THE STARS

In 1971, Chris Bell (pictured on the far left) formed Big Star with Alex Chilton. A hybrid of soul, pop and rock music, Big Star emerged as power-pop pioneers, yet their 1972 debut LP, *#1 Record*, sold fewer than 10,000 copies upon its release. Band relations were often fraught: Chilton had enjoyed chart success with The Box Tops' 1967 single, 'The Letter', so was already something of a star; Bell, meanwhile, felt threatened by Chilton's relative fame.

Leaving the group after the disappointment of their debut album, Bell battled with depression and a heroin dependency as he struggled to reconcile his sexuality and religious beliefs. While the Chilton-led group's commercial fortunes faltered still, Bell struggled with solo work, finally releasing the 'I Am The Cosmos'/'You And Your Sister' single in 1978. He died in a car crash later that year, on his way back from work at his father's East Memphis restaurant. His solo recordings were collected and released as *I Am The Cosmos* in 1992. Both Big Star and Bell's statures have continued to rise, with groups as diverse as REM and Primal Scream citing their influence.

DATE OF BIRTH

12 January 1951

DATE OF DEATH

27 December 1978

GENRES

Rock, pop-rock

ONLY THE
GOOD DIE YOUNG

JESSE BELVIN

MR EASY

Jesse Belvin recorded for many of the pioneering southern US R&B labels of the mid-to-late 1950s, including Special, Modern and Dot – finally signing to RCA, then home to Elvis Presley, in 1959. He also shared studio time with guitarist Johnny 'Guitar' Watson, a young Barry White and jazz saxophonist Art Pepper.

Despite such illustrious credentials, Belvin will forever be remembered for co-writing one of the most enduring doo-wop hits of the 1950s, the million-selling 'Earth Angel', recorded by The Penguins in 1954 and topping the *Billboard* R&B chart the following year. Belvin's greatest success under his own name was the No. 7 R&B hit, 'Goodnight My Love', released in 1956 and on which it's said an 11-year-old Barry White played piano.

By the time he signed to RCA, Belvin had earned the nickname 'Mr Easy'. After performing before the first-ever integrated white and black audience in Little Rock, Arkansas, Belvin and his wife were killed in a head-on car collision. Sam Cooke, also on the bill that night, continued to be influenced by Belvin's laid-back style.

DATE OF BIRTH

15 December 1932

DATE OF DEATH

6 February 1960

GENRES

R&B

THE BiG BOPPER

FROM TEXAS DJ TO ROCK'S FIRST XL PERSONALITY

Forever immortalized for answering the phone with a booming *'Hellooooooo baaaaaaaaaaaby!'* on No. 6 hit 'Chantilly Lace', The Big Bopper was one of rock'n'roll's first over-sized personalities. As a DJ for Texas' KTRM radio station, the man born Jiles Perry Richardson, Jr played the hottest single releases during R&B's early-to-mid-1950s heyday. After being drafted into the US Army in 1955 for two years, Richardson returned to the airwaves with a bang, breaking the world record for continuous on-air broadcasting when he played 1,821 records during one continuous broadcast from the Jefferson Theater in Baumont, Texas, lasting five days, two hours and eight minutes.

Richardson harboured songwriting ambitions, even penning No. 1 hits for George Jones ('White Lightning') and Johnny Preston ('Running Bear'). In 1958 he released 'Chantilly Lace' and its follow-up, 'The Big Bopper's Wedding', the successes of which took him out on tour with Buddy Holly, Ritchie Valens and Dion & The Belmonts. Two weeks into the tour, a combination of snowfall and a piloting error resulted in a fatal crash that killed the Bopper, Valens and Holly.

DATE OF BiRTH

24 October 1930

DATE OF DEATH

3 February 1959

GENRES

Rock'n'roll

ONLY THE
GOOD DiE YOUNG

MARC BOLAN

ELECTRIC WARRIOR

Having left school aged 15 to become a model, the man born Mark Feld in Hackney, London, would try an array of different musical styles before lighting glam rock's touch paper in 1970. After releasing a handful of solo singles in 1965 and 1966, including the chugging, beat-driven 'The Wizard' and acoustic-led 'Hippy Gumbo', Bolan was added by legendary impresario Simon Napier-Bell to the John's Children line-up. The group's chaotic live shows earned them a reputation as proto-punks, the myth stoked after they were kicked off of a supporting slot with The Who, while their debut single, 1967's 'Desdemona', was banned by the BBC.

Yet Bolan spent a mere four months with the infamous hellraisers, before falling out with Napier-Bell and returning to his hippy roots with Tyrannosaurus Rex, an acoustic duo formed with percussionist Steve Peregrin Took. Early LP releases such as 1968's *My People Were Fair And Had Sky In Their Hair... But Now They're Content To Wear Stars On Their Brows* and the following year's *Unicorn* attracted support from DJ John Peel, while also breaking into the UK Top 20. The recordings saw Bolan give free rein to his most fantastical poetry – the product of a creative mind that claimed he met a wizard while visiting Paris in 1965.

CHILDREN OF THE REVOLUTION

After relations soured with Took, Bolan hired Mickey Finn as replacement percussionist for Tyrannosaurus Rex's final album, 1970's *A Beard Of Stars*. Yet that wasn't the only change within the group: Bolan had begun adding electric instruments – a portent of what was to come.

In October 1970, just seven months after *A Beard Of Stars*, Bolan released 'Ride A White Swan', a UK No. 2 hit credited to T.Rex. The shortened name reflected the taut music the band was now creating: riff-driven pop songs that lost Bolan the support of John Peel, but gained him a worldwide following, invented glam rock and kick-started the onslaught of 'T.Rextacy' – a Beatlemania for the 1970s. Epochal albums followed, such as 1971's charting-topping *Electric Warrior* and the following year's *The Slider*, while Bolan enjoyed four No. 1 hits among a total of nine Top 5 single releases.

THE SLIDER

As Bolan's glam rock rival David Bowie reinvented himself with ever-more groundbreaking releases throughout the 1970s, Bolan remained content churning out riff-based songs to his established template. With the second half of the decade threatening to happen without him, Bolan's releases slid down the chart as punk and new wave started their gobby rise. Yet Bolan was in touch with the breakthrough bands, taking The Damned out on tour with him in 1977, and featuring Generation X on the final episode of his six-part TV show, *Marc*. Bolan would not see its 28 September broadcast. Driving home in the early hours of 16 September, after dining out with his girlfriend, Northern soul singer Gloria Jones, Jones lost control of the purple Mini the pair were travelling in, crashing it into a sycamore tree. Jones suffered severe injuries, while Bolan died upon impact.

DATE OF BIRTH

30 September 1947

DATE OF DEATH

16 September 1977

GENRES

Glam rock, hard rock

ONLY THE GOOD DIE YOUNG

TOMMY BOLIN

ETHEREAL ZEPHYR

Tommy Bolin's mastery of the guitar allowed him to deftly switch from blues playing to hard rock and jazz fusion, often within the same song. After cutting his teeth in local bands in and around his Sioux City, Iowa, birthplace, Bolin moved to Boulder, Colorado, making his mark as the standout musician with blues–rock five–piece Zephyr. Across the late 1960s and early 1970s, the group released three albums, 1969's self–titled debut, 1971's *Going Back To Colorado* and the following year's *Sunset Ride*, which failed to trouble the charts, but gained the guitarist a following.

After Zephyr dissolved, Bolin had a brief tenure with Billy Cobham's band, joining the ex–Mahavishnu Orchestra drummer for his solo debut, *Spectrum* – considered a landmark jazz fusion release. The union was brief, however, as Bolin was called upon to replace departing guitarist Domenic Troiano in hard rockers The James Gang. Despite spending barely a year as part of the Gang, Bolin managed to give their fading fortunes a boost on the 1973 album *Bang*, and its 1974 follow–up, *Miami*. Leaving The James Gang after touring the latter LP, Bolin spent a year performing both session and live work with a variety of rock and jazz acts, while also focusing on his own solo material.

PURPLE PATCH

The guitarist's debut solo album *Teaser* came out on Atlantic subsidiary Nemperor in 1975. A critical success praised for Bolin's commanding use of various musical styles, it failed to make much of a commercial impact. While recording the LP,

Bolin had been contacted by Deep Purple to fill the shoes of the legendary Ritchie Blackmore. Accepting the offer, Bolin subsequently found himself unable to promote his own solo album, as recording sessions and a tour with the rock behemoths beckoned.

It might have been Bolin's highest-profile gig, but Deep Purple were in turmoil. The fruits of the guitarist's work with the group, *Come Taste The Band*, failed to break the Top 40, despite going for a commercially friendly hard rock sound, tempered with funk overtones courtesy of the new recruit. Deep Purple split in March 1976 following a show at Liverpool's Empire Theatre. The Mk IV line-up of the group had lasted less than 12 months.

PRIVATE ON PARADE

Able to focus on his own material once again, Bolin took to the road with his own band, while working on his second solo album in the studio. Another critical success, *Private Eyes* was released on major label Columbia in September 1976. Touring in support of the album, he featured as opening act for Jeff Beck. On 4 December 1976, the day after a performance in Miami, Bolin's girlfriend found the guitarist unconscious in his hotel room. Having struggled with drug use for much of his career, his body gave out under a mix of heroin, cocaine, alcohol and barbiturates, just as Bolin's name was truly beginning to take off.

DATE OF BIRTH

1 August 1951

DATE OF DEATH

4 December 1976

GENRES

Hard rock, heavy metal

ONLY THE
GOOD DIE YOUNG

JOHN BONHAM

BIG BEAT MANIFESTO

One of the greatest rock musicians of all time, John Bonham was the complete package. A drummer with incredible speed and power, he was also blessed with a musicality lacking in many lesser kit-pounding tub-thumpers. Having started his career aged five, looking to jazz percussionists such as Buddy Rich, the nascent rock star graduated to his first full kit 10 years later. Following stints in a number of Birmingham-based bands, Bonham met future Led Zeppelin vocalist Robert Plant in blues group The Crawling King Snakes.

Over in London, celebrated blues boom pioneers The Yardbirds were on the skids. Having seen future guitar heroes Eric Clapton and Jeff Beck pass through their ranks, Jimmy Page was at the helm, though he was finding himself bored with the group's limitations. Enlisting bassist John Paul Jones for a new project, Page also convinced Robert Plant to join, bringing an initially reluctant John Bonham with him.

TRAMPLED UNDERFOOT

Briefly trading as The New Yardbirds, the four-piece settled on the name Led Zeppelin, finding initial success with audience-strafing live shows on the US West Coast. Their self-titled debut album came out in 1969, reaching the Top 10 on both sides of the Atlantic. It unleashed a blues-influenced, proto-heavy metal sound with classic recordings such as 'Dazed And Confused' and 'Communication Breakdown'. Plant's theatrical vocals and Page's stunning guitar work sat atop the sturdy rhythm section of Bonham and Jones, underpinned by the drummer's kit-work.

The group's following two albums, the same year's *Led Zeppelin II* (featuring the drum solo 'Moby Dick', often played live as a half-hour workout) and 1970's *Led Zeppelin III*, topped the charts on both sides of the Atlantic. In 1971, their celebrated fourth album (officially untitled, though often referred to as 'IV' or 'Four Symbols') built upon the folk-rock sound explored on *III*, and contained Led Zeppelin's most famous number, 'Stairway To Heaven'.

IN THROUGH THE OUT DOOR

Spending most of the 1970s as the biggest live act in the world, studio releases such as 1973's *Houses Of The Holy* and 1975's *Presence* ensured that Led Zeppelin were also hailed as one of the most inventive bands of the decade. Subsequent albums would, however, draw mixed reviews, and – like many stadium rock acts – Led Zeppelin would struggle to remain relevant as punk groups claimed 1977 for their Year Zero.

Having refrained from playing the UK since 1975, the group staged two homecoming shows at Knebworth in August 1979. A summer 1980 European tour followed, during which Bonham was hospitalized after collapsing on stage in Germany. A life of heavy drinking was taking its toll. During September rehearsals for a US tour, Bonham spent an entire day drinking – kicking off with four quadruple vodkas for breakfast – before asphyxiating on his own vomit in his sleep that night.

Since Bonham's death, Led Zeppelin have performed together a mere four times, including an appearance at Live Aid, with Phil Collins behind the kit, while John's son Jason has assumed his father's role for one-off performances such as 2007's Ahmet Ertegun Tribute Concert at London's O_2 Arena.

DATE OF BIRTH

31 May 1948

DATE OF DEATH

25 September 1980

GENRES

Hard rock, heavy metal

CLIFFORD BROWN
ILL-FATED HARD BOP PIONEER

Clifford 'Brownie' Brown seemed doomed from the start. Aged just 20, he suffered such horrendous injuries from a car crash in 1950 that he was hospitalized for a year. Yet pioneering bebop trumpeter Dizzy Gillespie visited Brown in hospital, convincing the young musician to pursue a full-time musical career. After his release from hospital, Brown developed an astoundingly fast playing style, perfect for the hard bop movement.

After apprenticing with the likes of big band leader Lionel Hampton and future Jazz Messenger Art Blakey, Brown formed The Clifford Brown & Max Roach Quartet: an apogee of hard bop playing propelled by Roach's pioneering melodic drumming style. Notable for never succumbing to the drug addictions that blighted the careers of many of his contemporaries, Brown still only remained professionally active for four years. Tragically, aged just 25, he, pianist Richard Powell and Powell's wife were fatally injured in another serious car accident in 1956. A career taking in performances with the likes of Sarah Vaughan and Sonny Rollins had only just begun to hint at what might have been possible for the trumpeter.

DATE OF BIRTH

30 October 1930

DATE OF DEATH

26 June 1956

GENRES

Bebop, hard bop

JEFF BUCKLEY

THERE BUT FOR THE GRACE

For an artist who only released one studio album, Jeff Buckley's legacy looms larger than that of many musicians with more extensive discographies. With acclaimed (but absent) singer–songwriter Tim Buckley for a father, a classically trained musician for a mother and a stepfather with a wide–ranging record collection, Buckley absorbed musical influences like a sponge. Aged 19, and following a disappointing year studying at Hollywood's Musician's Institute, the fledgling musician spent the second half of the 1980s employed in menial work while performing various styles of music with a slew of bands.

In 1991, Buckley performed four of his father's songs at the Greetings From Tim Buckley tribute event in New York City, his first major live appearance. Subsequently relocating to the East Coast, Buckley began working with ex–Magic Band member Gary Lucas. After a number of solo performances in various New York clubs, he found a regular slot at the famed Sin–é coffee house, where – with just his electric guitar and an astonishing, four–octave voice – Buckley developed original material alongside covers of artists as diverse as Nina Simone, Bob Dylan, Led Zeppelin and Nusrat Fateh Ali Khan. (Recordings from these performances would form his debut release, the 1993 *Live At Sin-é* EP; an expanded 10th–anniversary edition added further gems.)

EVERYBODY HERE WANTS YOU

As news of the transcendent Sin–é performances spread, Buckley found himself courted by a host of record labels, eventually signing with Colombia. Entering the studio with a newly assembled band and Nirvana producer Andy Wallace, Buckley recorded *Grace*. Among beautifully crafted original songs such as 'Last Goodbye', 'Lover, You Should've Come Over' and 'Dream Brother', there were definitive covers of 'Lilac Wine' and Leonard Cohen's 'Hallelujah'.

ONLY THE
GOOD DIE YOUNG

Though reaching a dismal No. 149 in the US charts (peaking at a much more respectable No. 50 in the UK), the 1994 album has been a perennial favourite of critics and fans alike. Buckley took his band on the road for most of 1995 and into 1996, proving to be an electrifying live performer; a reputation posthumously stoked by a number of live album releases, including 2000's *Mystery White Boy* and 2009's *Grace Around The World*.

LAST GOODBYE

Back in New York City, Buckley hired ex-Television frontman Tom Verlaine to produce his follow-up album. However, Buckley was unsatisfied with the results and retreated to Memphis in February to work on new material in solitude. Renting a tiny house in which to demo more songs, the musician also began playing low-profile shows at the local bar, Barristers.

Buckley's band flew to Memphis on 29 May 1997, in preparation for more recording sessions. While they were in the air, Jeff took to the waters, swimming in Wolf River Harbour fully clothed while singing along to the radio. As a tugboat passed by, friend and roadie Keith Foti, sitting on the riverbank, moved the radio and a guitar away from the water, only to turn back and see that Buckley had vanished. The singer's body was found six days later, having been pulled into the boat's slipstream.

DATE OF BIRTH

17 November 1966

DATE OF DEATH

29 May 1997

GENRES

Alternative rock, folk-rock

ONLY THE
GOOD DIE YOUNG

TIM BUCKLEY

STARSAILOR

One of the most ambitious singer–songwriters of the twentieth century, Tim Buckley was exposed to jazz and country music at an early age. His adolescent years coincided with the folk music revival of the early 1960s, during which Buckley formed one of his first groups, The Bohemians, with high–school friend Larry Beckett. While at school, he also met his future wife, Mary Guibert, to whom the singer would remain married for just a year, fathering future musician Jeff Buckley.

Divorcing his pregnant wife to live the troubadour's life, Buckley was spotted playing in LA by impresario Herb Cohen, who secured the singer a residency at the Night Owl Café in New York's folk hotbed, Greenwich Village. While in New York, Buckley found an ally in Lee Underwood, with whom he would form a life–long musical partnership.

BUZZIN' FLY

Soon signed to iconic West Coast label Elektra, Buckley released his 1966 self–titled debut at the age of 19. Indebted to the folk–rock of the era, it gave Buckley the foundation on which to build the following year's more ambitious *Goodbye And Hello*. As his name grew, so did Buckley's refusal to play the fame game. Uncommunicative during television appearances planned to raise his profile, he was far more concerned with following his artistic muse. 1969's *Happy Sad* saw Buckley assimilate jazz influences into his folk–rock template. It was Buckley's most commercially successful album, but marked the point at which he left the mainstream path for the next few years.

ONLY THE
GOOD DIE YOUNG

Within 12 months of *Happy Sad*'s release, Buckley issued *Blue Afternoon* on the Frank Zappa–backed Straight imprint and *Lorca* through Elektra, the former relying on older material, the latter charting the musician's journey deeper into the avant–garde. Neither sold well, but both paved the way for Buckley's defining artistic statement, 1970's *Starsailor*. Including his most famous recording, the deceptively simple, intensely beautiful 'Song To The Siren', the album was by far Buckley's most ambitious work. Assimilating all his past influences into one indefinable whole, the singer fully harnessed the power of using his own voice like an instrument, setting the stage for the vocal acrobatics performed by his son two decades later.

LOOK AT THE FOOL

After such a stunning blast of creativity in such a short period, Buckley spent his remaining years seemingly artistically spent, disappearing into drink and drug binges while his commercial fortunes refused to pick up. 1972's *Greetings From LA* mined an overtly sexual funk groove, but the response was cool, and the following year's *Sefronia* and 1974's *Look At The Fool* left a small audience eager for the musician's more experimental works unmoved. Faced with dwindling sales, Buckley began playing older material onstage to try to revive his flagging career. Closing a 1975 stint of touring with a weekend binge, the singer ended up arguing with a friend after looking to score some heroin from him. After ingesting all he was given, Buckley was taken home to recover, later dying of an overdose on his living room floor.

DATE OF BIRTH

14 February 1947

DATE OF DEATH

29 June 1975

GENRES

Folk, experimental rock

ONLY THE
GOOD DIE YOUNG

JOHNNY BURNETTE

BOXING CLEVER

Growing up in the same Memphis housing project as Elvis Presley, Johnny Burnette appeared to be set for a sports career, earning places in Memphis Catholic High School's baseball and football teams. Taking up boxing alongside his older brother Dorsey in the late 1940s, Johnny would go on to become a lightweight Golden Gloves champion, while his brother won the accolade in the welterweight division.

Though he had to give up on a professional fighting career after suffering a broken nose during a match, the boxing world framed one of Johnny's most important meetings: in 1949, the Burnette brothers forged a friendship with fellow Golden Gloves competitor Paul Burlison. The latter had spent time in the US Navy, earning an honourable discharge the year he met the Burnettes. Meanwhile, Johnny and Dorsey had been working menial jobs on the Mississippi River, playing guitar in their spare time and accumulating a repertoire of songs, which they would perform in local bars when on land.

POWER RANGERS

Forming a solid three-piece, with Burlison on lead guitar, Dorsey on bass and Johnny singing, the three ex-boxers moved to New York in 1956 – the year Elvis Presley became a nationwide sensation. As The Rhythm Rangers, the trio won Ted Mack's *Original Amateur Hour* three consecutive times, earning themselves a contract with the Coral imprint, future home to rock'n'roll pioneer Buddy Holly. Having renamed themselves The Rock'n'Roll Trio, the group began promoting singles recorded with their distinctively clipped, treble-heavy rockabilly sound. But the singles weren't selling, and the brothers started fighting and Johnny Burnette & The Rock'n'Roll Trio – as they were contentiously being billed – began falling apart.

ONLY THE
GOOD DIE YOUNG

Dorsey quit the group later in the year and was replaced by Johnny Black, brother of Elvis's bassist Bill. Meanwhile, the trio had added Carl Perkins' cousin Tony Austin as a drummer. A hit single failed to materialize, however, and the revamped Rock'n'Roll Trio found themselves strung out on the road, tiring of the endless grind. By the time 'If You Want It Enough' was released in December 1957, the group had decided that it did not and disbanded.

LONESOME TRAIN (ON A LONESOME TRACK)

Johnny reunited with Dorsey in California and the pair made another stab at fame, releasing a handful of non-charting singles as a duo. Striking out as a solo artist on Liberty, Johnny finally found success in 1959, going on to achieve his biggest hit the following year, when 'You're Sixteen' charted at No. 8 in the US and entered the Top 3 in the UK. A ruptured appendix stalled his momentum, however, and further releases, though respectable, failed to reach such heights.

As the British Invasion began taking hold, Burnette's singles struggled to make the charts. In August 1964 – with the singer having failed to chart for 12 months – a cabin cruiser collided with Burnette's fishing boat, knocking him overboard. Burnette drowned, never living long enough to see the acclaim his original band would receive. Their sole LP, 1956's *Johnny Burnette And The Rock'n'Roll Trio*, has been hailed as one of the pioneering rockabilly releases of the 1950s.

DATE OF BIRTH

25 March 1934

DATE OF DEATH

14 August 1964

GENRES

Rockabilly

CLIFF BURTON

THERE IS NO JUSTICE

Assimilating classical, prog, punk and heavy metal styles, Cliff Burton elevated the bass from rhythmic instrument – underpinning a melody and driving a song forward – to the status of a lead when he joined thrash metal pioneers Metallica at the age of 20.

Winning a local battle of the bands competition in Hayward, California, with his second band, Agents Of Misfortune, and showcasing material that he would later record with Metallica, Burton took his third band, Trauma, to Los Angeles for a live engagement at the famed Sunset Strip venue, the Whisky a Go Go. Metallica's guitarist/singer James Hetfield and drummer Lars Ulrich caught Trauma's set, immediately thinking that Burton's fast, intricate playing was lead guitar work. Finding out that he was a bass player, and eager to poach him for their own group, Metallica agreed to move north from LA to El Cerrito, in order to accommodate Burton's living arrangements.

THE FOUR HORSEMEN

After sacking lead guitarist (and future Megadeth founder) Dave Mustaine, whose substance abuse was rendering him increasingly difficult to work with, Metallica and replacement guitarist Kirk Hammett relocated to New Jersey to record their debut album for the Megaforce imprint. 1983's *Kill 'Em All* (a title coined by Burton in response to stockists' wariness of the band's original title choice: *Metal Up Your Ass*) was a groundbreaking album combining elements of the New Wave Of British Heavy Metal, punk and speed metal, ushering in the new thrash metal movement. The instrumental track '(Anesthesia) Pulling Teeth' was a Burton showcase, in which the bassist unleashed the solo that caught Hetfield and

ONLY THE
GOOD DIE YOUNG

Ulrich's attention in LA, replete with his innovative playing of a bass guitar through a wah-wah pedal. The follow-up album, 1984's *Ride The Lightning*, built upon this template, introducing even more complex and ambitious song arrangements and breaking the US Top 100.

FADE TO BLACK

Signing to major label Elektra for their third LP, 1986's *Master Of Puppets*, Metallica consolidated everything they had accomplished on their previous two albums to produce a work hailed as one of the most important metal albums of all time. Without any promotional radio play to support it, *Puppets* sold over three million copies and peaked at No. 29 in the US charts (No. 44 in the UK).

It would, however, be their last album with Burton. While on the road in support of the release, the group bemoaned the lack of comfort on their tour bus. Following a concert in Stockholm, Burton and Hammett drew cards to see who got first choice of the on-board sleeping cubicles. Burton won and claimed the best bed. In the early morning, the bus skidded off the road, throwing Burton through the window before flipping and landing on top of him. The group chose to continue with replacement bassist Jason Newsted. Now one of the biggest metal bands in the planet, Metallica have released five No. 1 albums, beginning with 1991's *Metallica*, while also releasing a high-profile collaboration with Lou Reed, 2011's *Lulu*.

DATE OF BIRTH

10 February 1962

DATE OF DEATH

27 September 1986

GENRES

Heavy metal, hard rock

ONLY THE
GOOD DIE YOUNG

KAREN CARPENTER

A FAMILY AFFAIR

Enlisting in Downey High School after moving from Connecticut to Los Angeles with her family, Karen Carpenter joined the school band, occupying the drummer's stool after finding herself dissatisfied playing the glockenspiel. In the mid–1960s, she began playing with her pianist brother, releasing 500 copies of the 'Looking For Love'/'I'll Be Yours' single – credited solely to Karen – on the independent Magic Lamp imprint in 1966.

Live engagements as The Richard Carpenter Trio with Wes Jacobs kept the brother-and-sister team occupied on the jazz circuit, though studio recordings as Spectrum – focusing on a group vocal sound – failed to gain the interest of record labels. During this time, Karen received medical advice recommending the high–protein/low–carbohydrate Stillman Diet, resulting in a notable loss of weight over the coming years.

WE'VE ONLY JUST BEGUN

The Santa Monica–based A&M record label finally picked up on the pair, signing them as The Carpenters and releasing their debut album, *Offering*, in 1969. It failed to make much of a mark, though a cover of The Beatles' 'Ticket To Ride' peaked at No. 54 in the singles charts. The following year's *Closer To You*, however, included a chart–topping cover of the almost–title track, '(They Long To Be) Close To You' and the No. 2 hit 'We've Only Just Begun', both definitive recordings that brought the duo's to a mainstream audience.

The first half of the 1970s remained The Carpenters' decade. Albums such as 1972's *Carpenters*, the following year's *A Song For You* and 1974's *Now & Then* all entered the Top 5 in the US, while the last peaked at No. 2 on both sides of the Atlantic. Their singles success was a little more erratic, although most entered the Top 10, and many found places in the Top 3.

Sales faltered throughout the remainder of the decade, yet The Carpenters remained a popular draw, appearing on a number of one-off television specials. Come 1979, however, Richard took a year-long sabbatical from the group to recover from a Quaaludes addiction. During this time, Karen recorded a solo album, but it was at odds with The Carpenters' soft rock and the uptempo, disco-tinged music was rejected by A&M.

AS TIME GOES BY

As the 1980s dawned, The Carpenters seemed out of step with the times. *Made In America*, and most of its attendant singles, failed to break the Top 50. Having been dieting since her teens, Karen – now in her 30s – was severely anorexic. She was also going through a stressful divorce and seeking psychotherapeutic help. In 1983, she suffered heart failure at her parents' house.

There has been both enough material in the vault – and high demand for The Carpenters' easy-going music – to result in a number of posthumous collections of unreleased recordings over the years, while Karen's solo album finally saw the light of day in 1996. Richard went on to release two solo albums, 1987's *Time* and 1998's *Pianist, Arranger, Composer, Conductor*, while maintaining The Carpenters' legacy.

DATE OF BIRTH

2 March 1950

DATE OF DEATH

4 February 1983

GENRES

Pop

ONLY THE
GOOD DIE YOUNG

ARLESTER 'DYKE' CHRISTIAN

PROTO-FUNK TRAILBLAZER

From birth, Arlester Christian's story has been shrouded in mystery. It is generally accepted that he was born in Buffalo, New York, in 1943, and began playing bass, aged 17, with Carl LaRue & His Crew. After travelling to Phoenix for a failed engagement with an early incarnation of The O'Jays in 1965, Christian stayed on and hooked up with local group The Three Blazers, forming Dyke & The Blazers and pioneering a raw streak of proto-funk.

Released in 1967, 'Funky Broadway' became a *Billboard* Hot Soul Singles chart-topper, while also marking the first appearance of the word 'funky' in any song title. It kicked off a peak period of recording for the group, which lasted until 1969 (and included the No. 4 R&B hit 'Let A Woman Be A Woman, Let A Man Be A Man'). The Blazers' commercial success waned as the 1970s dawned, however, and Christian – set to tour England and record with Barry White – was shot dead in the street in March 1971. Rumours that he had links with drug dealing remain unfounded.

DATE OF BIRTH

13 June 1943

DATE OF DEATH

13 March 1971

GENRES

R&B, funk

ONLY THE
GOOD DIE YOUNG

STEVE CLARK

NWOBHM'S FIRST-WAVE RIFFMASTER

Nicknamed 'The Riffmaster' by Def Leppard vocalist Joe Elliott, Steve Clark took up the guitar aged 11 and joined the Sheffield-based New Wave Of British Heavy Metal legends as their second lead guitarist, just seven years later, in 1978. Def Leppard's live popularity led to a record deal with legendary UK label Vertigo, and debut album *On Through The Night* followed in 1980.

It wasn't until 1987 and the release of their fourth album, *Hysteria*, that Def Leppard achieved worldwide success. A No. 1 smash on both sides of the Atlantic, seven of the album's 12 tracks were released as singles, including the hard-rock mainstay 'Pour Some Sugar On Me'. Recording sessions for the album's follow-up (*Adrenalize*, another transatlantic chart-topper when it was released in 1992) were hampered by Clark's escalating alcohol dependency, as the guitarist was spending an increasing amount of time in rehab. After being given a six-month leave of absence from the group in the middle of 1990, Clark ingested a cocktail of prescription drugs and alcohol the following January. His subsequent overdose was accidental, though tragically fatal.

DATE OF BIRTH

23 April 1960

DATE OF DEATH

8 January 1991

GENRES

Heavy metal, hard rock

ONLY THE
GOOD DIE YOUNG

PATSY CLINE

COUNTRY MUSIC'S FIRST FEMALE STAR

The first female solo artist inducted into the Country Music Hall Of Fame, Virginia Patterson Hensley spent her teenage years working menial jobs to help her family, which had been abandoned by her father when she was 15. That same year, 1947, she approached the DJ of local radio station WINC–AM to ask if she could sing on air. The response to her appearance was so great that Cline was invited back for repeat performances, and the singer started to book gigs on the local Winchester, Virginia, live circuit. By the mid–1950s, she had become a regular fixture singing country music both on the radio and in nightclubs.

Marrying in 1953, Cline was divorced just four years later. She had signed to the Four Star imprint in 1955 as Patsy Cline, releasing a handful of non–charting singles (including her aptly titled debut, 'A Church, A Courtroom, And Goodbye').

CRAZY FOR LOVING YOU

Now performing before a national audience via appearances on the *Grand Ole Opry*, Cline seemed content to sing country music, dressed in her mother's handmade fringed cowgirl outfits. For her high–profile appearance on *Arthur Godfrey's Talent Scouts*, however, the show's producers dressed Cline in a cocktail dress, giving her 'Walkin' After Midnight' to sing – a song Cline thought was too pop for her style. The performance was a smash, however, and a recorded version became her breakout hit, reaching No. 2 in the country charts and No. 12 in the pop charts – one of the first ever country crossover hits.

Despite releasing a further 12 singles over four years, Cline, limited to recording material written by the Four Star house team, failed to enter the charts a second time in the 1950s. During those four years, however, she married her second – and life-long – husband, Charlie Dick, and found a new manager, Randy Hughes. Signing with Decca in 1960, Cline was teamed with Owen Bradley – one of the progenitors of the early 1960s Nashville sound – who knew how to get the best out the singer's voice.

FALL TO PIECES

Released in 1961, 'I Fall To Pieces' reached No. 1 in the country charts. Its follow-up, 'Crazy', peaked at No. 2, and the following year's 'She's Got You' returned Cline to the top spot. All three singles peaked high in the pop charts, too. Bradley's opulent string arrangements helped Cline become one of the most successful country–pop crossover musicians of the decade. Cline almost died in a car crash in 1961, though she recovered from her injuries, going out on tour the following year and becoming the first female country singer to perform a headline show.

Recording sessions for a fourth LP saw the singer edge towards an even more pronounced pop sound. Where Cline's career was headed will, however, remain forever unknown. Following a performance at a benefit concert in Kansas City, March 1963, Cline died in a plane crash while travelling home. Her manager had been at the controls, but lost control of the aircraft after flying into severe weather conditions.

DATE OF BIRTH

8 September 1932

DATE OF DEATH

5 March 1963

GENRES

Nashville sound, country, traditional pop

ONLY THE
GOOD DIE YOUNG

KURT COBAIN

TEEN SPIRIT

Along with Pearl Jam and Mudhoney, Nirvana were leading lights of Seattle's mid-1980s grunge scene, helping to take the music overground with their phenomenal early-1990s success. Frontman Kurt Cobain and bassist Krist Novoselic formed the three-piece group in 1987. Unable to find a permanent drummer, the group were on their fifth sticksman, Chad Channing, before recording their debut single, 1988's 'Love Buzz'.

Taking his inspiration from late-1980s alt-rock pioneers The Pixies, Cobain's songwriting followed that group's loud-quiet-loud dynamics, but with a melodic sensibility that gave way to traditional song structures underneath the aggressive sound. Debut album *Bleach* failed to enter the charts upon its initial release, however, as Cobain's songs leant more towards the abrasive, in an attempt to fit in on legendary local indie label Sub Pop.

RADIO FRIENDLY UNIT SHIFTER

Following a tour in support of *Bleach*, the group began working on new material, but found themselves again looking for a drummer. They found Dave Grohl of local hardcore act Scream. The group's new material was poppier than before and Nirvana began looking for a major label record deal, signing with Geffen subsidiary DGC. The first fruits of this new arrangement, 'Smells Like Teen Spirit', became a Top 10 hit on both sides of the Atlantic, while its parent album *Nevermind*, released two weeks later on 24 September 1991, topped the charts in the US and reached No. 5 in the UK. After undertaking one exhausting tour for the album, the group made select high-profile shows in 1992, including a career-defining performance at England's Reading Festival.

ONLY THE
GOOD DIE YOUNG

Having attained mainstream success, Cobain soon found the pressures of fame taking their toll. He was also due to become a father in August 1992, following his marriage to Hole frontwoman Courtney Love. With a heroin addiction exacerbating his troubles, Cobain set to work on the group's third album. Recorded with fewer overdubs than *Nevermind*, and with Pixies producer Steve Albini, *In Utero* was less radio-friendly than its predecessor, though it entered the charts at No. 1 when it was released in September 1993.

I HATE MYSELF AND WANT TO DIE

Cobain had originally wanted to call the record *I Hate Myself And Want To Die*. Setting out on tour as a four-piece with The Germs' Pat Smear on guitar, Cobain's drug addiction began spiralling out of control. He had already overdosed on heroin in July 1993 and, in March the following year, overdosed on a mix of champagne and Rohypnol. The remainder of the tour was cancelled. By the end of the month – after an incident involving pills and a gun – Love, friends and musicians intervened.

Cobain checked into LA's Exodus Recovery Center, only to walk out within days and fly back to Seattle. A week later, he committed suicide at home with a shotgun, quoting Neil Young in his suicide note: 'It's better to burn out than to fade away.' Posthumous releases, including *MTV Unplugged In New York* – lauded for unveiling the group's uncharacteristic acoustic arrangements – have kept Cobain's legacy alive. Dave Grohl went on to form The Foo Fighters, while Nirvana remain hailed as one of the greatest acts of their generation.

DATE OF BIRTH

20 February 1967

DATE OF DEATH

8 April 1994

GENRES

Alternative rock, grunge

ONLY THE
GOOD DIE YOUNG

EDDIE COCHRAN

TWENTY FLIGHT ROCKER SOARS

In four short years as a recording artist, Eddie Cochran had as sizeable an impact on 1950s teenagers as his contemporary Elvis Presley. First learning guitar to perform the country music he heard on the radio as a child, Cochran could also play piano and began writing his own songs in school.

As Elvis Presley was enjoying mainstream success and performing in his first film, *Love Me Tender*, Cochran appeared in the 1956 film *The Girl Can't Help It* alongside pioneers Gene Vincent and Little Richard. Yet while Elvis sang a more subdued title track compared to the rock'n'roll he was famous for, Cochran's raucous performance of 'Twenty Flight Rock' marked the first time that many teenagers would have seen rock'n'roll in the movies. Future Beatle Paul McCartney was so influenced by Cochran's role that he played the song to John Lennon, subsequently gaining entry into Lennon's first band, The Quarrymen.

SUMMERTIME BLOOMS

Cochran released two singles the following year. 'Sittin' In The Balcony' – a paean to cinema dates in the dark – made it to No. 8 in February, though the similarly themed 'Drive In Show' limped to No. 82 five months later. In November that year, *Singin' To My Baby* came out. The only LP release during Cochran's lifetime, it saw his record label attempt to smooth the singer's sound for a more pop-oriented audience.

Despite this, Cochran's fourth single was another rave-up. Perfectly timed for release in July 1958, 'Summertime Blues' became his biggest-charting hit, peaking at No. 8. Capturing the frustrations of 1950s teenagers around the world,

the song saw Cochran bemoan having to work during his summer holidays, while adults refused to listen to his complaints. An evergreen rock'n'roll staple, The Beach Boys, proto-heavy metal act Blue Cheer and The Who all recorded their own versions of the song.

TEENAGE HEAVEN

Shaken by news of the plane crash that killed Buddy Holly, Cochran became reluctant to tour, though an invite to the UK in 1960 was too good an offer to turn down. Cochran took to the road with his former *The Girl Can't Help It* co-star Gene Vincent, while his girlfriend and songwriter, Sharon Sheeley, flew out to England to be with him. (Sheeley co-wrote Cochran's final single release, the No. 58-charting 1959 release 'Somethin' Else'.)

While travelling through Wiltshire in a speeding taxi, the vehicle blew a tyre and the driver lost control. Cochran tried to shield Sheeley from harm, but flew out of the car himself after it crashed into a lamppost. Despite being rushed to hospital, Cochran's head injuries were so severe that he died in the early hours of the following morning. Cochran's girlfriend survived the crash, going on to write songs with both Jackie DeShannon and The Searchers. Gene Vincent also survived, but damaged his leg so badly that he remained permanently impaired, adding to an iconic image, as eulogized in Ian Dury's song 'Sweet Gene Vincent'.

DATE OF BIRTH

3 October 1938

DATE OF DEATH

17 April 1960

GENRES

Rock'n'roll

SAM COOKE

MR SOUL

Like many soul performers of the 1960s, Sam Cooke began singing gospel music, going on to join The Soul Stirrers in the early 1950s. Making a number of religious recordings for the Specialty imprint, the singer built up a large following. For his first solo single, 1956's 'Lovable', however, Cooke used the pseudonym 'Dale Cook', hoping to avoid disappointing his religious fan-base with secular material.

Moving to the Keen label the following year, Sam released 'You Send Me' – a No. 1 hit in both the R&B and pop charts. Though he continued to record crossover material – including '(I Love You) For Sentimental Reasons' and a cover of George Gershwin's 'Summertime' – Cooke spent the remainder of the decade achieving greater success in the R&B market.

BRING IT ON HOME

Cooke's pioneering mix of R&B, gospel and pop music has often seen him credited with inventing soul music – an honour acknowledged with the title of his 1963 album, *Mr Soul*. Launching his own SAR label in 1961 – becoming one of the first black artists to take charge of his own business concerns – Cooke also gave fledging soul artists such as Bobby Womack important boosts early in their careers. 'Chain Gang', meanwhile, became another huge hit for the singer when it peaked at No. 2 in both the pop and R&B charts in 1960. The following year's 'Cupid' only made the Top 20 in both charts, but has become one of Cooke's most enduring songs.

Whereas many R&B singers were most notable for their single releases in the early 1960s, Sam Cooke also created noteworthy LPs. Though only reaching No. 62 in 1963, *Night Beat* has been hailed as one of the greatest soul LPs

ONLY THE
GOOD DIE YOUNG

ever recorded, thanks in part to Cooke's masterfully controlled vocals and the music's sensitive arrangements. Recorded the same year – though not released until 1985 – *Live At The Harlem Square Club 1963* proved that the singer was a masterful live performer as well.

NiGHT BEAT

Cooke's murder has long been shrouded in mystery, the facts obscured by conflicting accounts of what happened on the night of 11 December 1964. What is undisputed is that the singer was shot to death in Los Angeles' Hacienda Motel by the establishment's manager, Bertha Franklin, and was found wearing just a jacket and his shoes. Franklin claimed that Cooke attacked her in the motel while drunk and looking for a woman that he had been with earlier. The manager said she shot him in self-defence. Cooke's guest, Elisa Boyer, also claimed to have been attacked by the singer. That thousands of dollars of cash was reportedly missing from his room has led to speculation that the singer was murdered in a conspiracy.

Just two weeks after the Cooke's death, 'A Change Is Gonna Come' was released as a single. Conceived as a black answer to Dylan's 'Blowin' In The Wind', the song quickly became an anthem for the Civil Rights Movement and the singer's defining artistic statement.

DATE OF BiRTH

22 January 1931

DATE OF DEATH

11 December 1964

GENRES

R&B, soul, gospel, pop, jazz

DARBY CRASH

LIVING FAST, DYING YOUNG EXEMPLIFIED

A pioneer of Los Angeles' hardcore LA punk scene, Jan Paul Beahm rechristened himself Darby Crash and co-founded The Germs with his friend Pat Smear in 1977, leading a four-piece group into punk's chaotic fray. Renowned for their live shows, The Germs frequently performed under the influence of drugs and alcohol, with Crash developing an alarming heroin addiction that often rendered him incoherent on stage.

The Germs' only album, *(GI)*, was released in 1979. It married Crash's manic, apocalyptic vision to Smear's musicality; produced by Joan Jett, it also blueprinted the future of LA punk. After Crash kicked drummer Don Bolles out of the band, The Germs imploded and Darby went on to form the short-lived Darby Crash Band. Failing to attract the interest that his former group did, a string of Germs reunion shows were subsequently organized. Crash used the money from them to buy enough heroin to kill himself, on 7 December 1980, aged just 22. John Lennon's murder the following day ultimately overshadowed Crash's final act. A reunited Germs, with Shane West in the frontman role, began touring in 2006.

DATE OF BIRTH

26 September 1958

DATE OF DEATH

7 December 1980

GENRES

Punk rock

JIM CROCE
STILL GOT A NAME

Jim Croce's reputation as the singer–songwriter's singer–songwriter continues to grow in stature. As a student at Philadelphia's Villanova University in the early 1960s, Croce formed a variety of bands to perform at coffee houses during the folk boom – even embarking on a small tour of Africa and the Middle East. Upon his return to Pennsylvania, Croce self-funded the release of his debut album, 1966's *Facets*, and met his future wife, Ingrid Jacobson.

Performing together, the couple relocated to New York to record 1969's *Croce*. Quickly tiring of both the city and the music industry, however, they moved back to the Pennsylvania countryside, where Jim took on menial employment to pay the bills while he wrote blue collar songs influenced by his day jobs. It was three years before he released another record, but 1972's pointedly titled *You Don't Mess Around With Jim* was quickly followed by 1973's *Life And Times* (featuring the No. 1 single 'Bad, Bad Leroy Brown') and *I Got A Name*. The day his 'I Got A Name' single was released, Croce died in a plane crash while on tour.

DATE OF BIRTH

10 January 1943

DATE OF DEATH

20 September 1973

GENRES

Folk–rock, folk, pop

ONLY THE
GOOD DIE YOUNG

IAN CURTIS

PIONEERING FUTURIST IN POST-PUNK FACTORY

Such is the legend of The Sex Pistols' July 1976 Manchester Free Trade Hall concert that almost everyone who was a youth in the city at that time claims to have witnessed it. Bassist Peter Hook and guitarist Bernard Sumner were two adolescents captivated by the group's performance that night. Forming a band immediately afterwards, they hired local boy Ian Curtis as vocalist, while running through a series of drummers before solidifying their line-up with Stephen Morris. Initially calling themselves The Stiff Kittens, the group renamed themselves Warsaw the following year, before settling on Joy Division, in reference to Jewish sex slaves imprisoned in Nazi concentration camps.

Quickly outgrowing their punk roots, Joy Division went on to embody the new wave/post-punk sound of the late 1970s and early 1980s. Independent Manchester label Factory signed the group following their self-released *An Ideal For Living* EP in 1978, and the band quickly became one of the iconic label's most defining acts.

THE SOUND OF MUSIC

Factory manager Tony Wilson had so much faith in Joy Division that he invested some of his inheritance into recording their debut album. Released in 1979, *Unknown Pleasures* was no runaway commercial success, but it quickly became one of the most influential albums of the twentieth century. The band members might have written the songs, but producer Martin Hannett honed a more spacious, atmospheric sound for them, at odds with the taut punk material prevalent at the time. With Peter Saville's simple but effective artwork, the album introduced Joy Division's mix of stark futurism to the world and put Factory on the map.

ONLY THE
GOOD DIE YOUNG

Performing live was a strain for Curtis, who suffered from epilepsy and would often go into seizure onstage. Almost an anti-frontman, he often appeared awkward in his own skin, suffering regularly from sleep deprivation brought on by his ill health. Audiences assumed it was part of the act, though the band grew increasingly concerned about their singer as 1980 dawned.

ATROCITY EXHIBITION

Following a tour of Europe, Joy Division took to the studio to work on their second album, *Closer*, in March 1980. Hannett again brought an inventive sonic backdrop to bear on the group's material, giving the finished recordings an elegiac tone to match song titles such as 'Atrocity Exhibition' and 'Isolation'. This time around, Curtis' lyrics were even more despairing; his health had worsened and his marriage to Deborah Curtis was also suffering, in part due to a close relationship the singer had begun to enjoy with Anik Honoré.

On the eve of a planned American tour in May and with divorce proceedings looming, Curtis was home alone. When Deborah returned the following morning, she found her husband hanged, having spent the night listening to Iggy Pop's LP *The Idiot*. Released the previous month, Joy Division's 'Love Will Tear Us Apart' single went on to become their biggest chart hit, reaching No. 13. *Closer* came out in July, a fitting requiem. That same month, Joy Division's remaining band members chose to continue as New Order, pioneering a strand of electro-pop throughout the 1980s.

DATE OF BIRTH

15 July 1956

DATE OF DEATH

18 May 1980

GENRES

Post-punk

PETE DE FREITAS

CUTTERED DOWN IN HIS PRIME

Liverpudlian new wave group Echo & The Bunnymen had been going for just a year when the Trinidad and Tobago–born drummer Pete de Freitas (pictured on the far right) joined them in 1979, advancing their drum machine–led sound in time for the Bunnymen's 1980 debut album, *Crocodiles*. The LP entered the Top 20, marking the beginning of a critically and commercially acclaimed career, which would see the group play the first WOMAD festival and release three Top 5 albums.

Crocodiles' follow-up, the No. 2 album *Porcupine*, contained The Bunnymen's first Top 10 song, 'The Cutter'. It was not until 1984's *Ocean Rain*, however, that the group realized their full potential with a groundbreaking album hailed as their defining artistic statement and including their masterpiece, 'The Killing Moon'. Such high aspirations were difficult to keep up with, however, and 1987's self-titled follow-up was a disappointment. Lead singer Ian McCulloch left the group the following year, while de Freitas was killed in a motorcycle accident on his way from London to Liverpool in 1989. A reformed Bunnymen began touring and recording sporadically throughout the late 1990s and 2000s, beginning with 1997's *Evergreen* album.

DATE OF BIRTH

2 August 1961

DATE OF DEATH

14 June 1989

GENRES

Post-punk

DO NOT FEED
THE SKELETONS

SANDY DENNY

BRITISH FOLK-ROCK LIEGE-END

Born in London, Denny learned traditional songs from her Scottish grandmother. She joined the UK capital's folk club circuit while studying at Kingston College of Art in the mid-1960s. Astonishingly prolific, Denny was performing on the BBC's *Folk Song Cellar* as early as 1966, while she made her first appearances on vinyl with the following year's *Alex Campbell And His Friends* and *Sandy And Johnny* LPs.

Following a brief stint with The Strawbs in 1968, Denny fell in with the doyens of British folk-rock, Fairport Convention, who were then looking for a new singer. With Denny's knowledge of folk music and the group's inventive electric instrument-led arrangements, their three 1969 albums, *What We Did On Our Holidays*, *Unhalfbricking* and *Liege & Lief*, went on to define modern folk-rock in the late 1960s.

NORTH STAR WANDERER

Leaving Fairport Convention to focus on her own music, Denny formed Fotheringay in 1970. Their self-titled debut came out in the summer of that year, with Denny receiving a writing credit on over half of the material. The short-lived group disbanded in 1971 while working on their second album, with recordings from those sessions being released as *Fotheringay 2* in 2008.

Denny's first solo album proper, 1971's *The North Star Grassman And The Ravens*, featured only three covers among its 11 tracks. Denny's arrangements were becoming more ambitious than before, and her lyrics couched in metaphor,

and she also began taking more control over the production of her records. The following year's *Sandy* arguably marked her early-1970s folk-rock peak, while 1974's *Like An Old Fashioned Waltz* eschewed traditional songs, as Denny assimilated jazz influences into her music.

MEET ON THE LEDGE

Despite moving away from her folk-rock roots, Denny reunited with Fairport Convention at the end of 1973, touring with the group and capturing the results on 1974's *Fairport Live Convention*. The brief reunion also yielded the following year's *Rising For The Moon* studio LP – an album recorded by a mix of then-current Fairport and ex-Fotheringay musicians.

Rising For The Moon failed to enter the Top 50, so Denny returned to the studio to record her own *Rendezvous* LP. Husband and former Fotheringay guitarist Trevor Lucas gave the record a contemporary sheen, but his production served to bury the quality of the songs, not enhance them. Listeners could not fail to hear the deterioration in Denny's voice, either. Heavy drinking and smoking had weakened one of her greatest assets; cocaine abuse added to her problems; and, after giving birth to a daughter in 1977, Denny started behaving even more erratically.

After falling down some stairs while on holiday with her parents in March 1978, the singer began experiencing severe headaches. Adding painkillers to her list of ingested substances, Denny collapsed a few weeks later, suffering a brain haemorrhage and falling into a coma, before dying in hospital. Her legacy continues to grow, however, not least with a string of posthumous releases doubling her discography, and Denny is now hailed as a towering UK songwriting talent.

DATE OF BIRTH

6 January 1947

DATE OF DEATH

21 April 1978

GENRES

Folk-rock

ONLY THE
GOOD DIE YOUNG

NiCK DRAKE

MADE TO LOVE MAGIC

Nick Drake's enigmatic image has been enhanced over the years thanks to a lack of video footage of the musician. In an era where most archive performance footage gets exhumed for the completists, still photos have remained all that exists to conjure the singer. Those and the music: three albums, released over four years, the impact of which reverberate through singer-songwriters today.

While at public school, Drake captained the rugby team – perhaps the most extroverted he had ever been in his life. Interest in music soon took over, however, and the fledgling performer began playing standards and contemporary hits with school friends, under the decidedly delicate name The Perfumed Gardeners. Following a stint travelling and experimenting with drugs, Drake went up to Cambridge University, though he was happier performing in coffee houses than attending lectures.

HANGING ON A STAR

Fairport Convention bassist Ashley Hutchings became enamoured with Drake, introducing him to Fairport and Incredible String Band producer Joe Boyd. Equally impressed with the student's music, Boyd offered to record Drake's debut LP. Backed by the cream of the UK's folk musicians, from Fairport Convention and Pentangle, Drake recorded *Five Leaves Left* over 12 months. The results, released in 1969, revealed an ambitious merging of Drake's low-key songs and folk-rock backing, with school friend Robert Kirby's dramatic string arrangements. The response was muted.

Leaving university for a full-time career in music, Drake returned to the studio with Boyd and Fairport musicians, plus ex-Velvet Underground multi-instrumentalist John Cale, to record 1970's *Bryter Later*. A wider musical

ONLY THE GOOD DIE YOUNG

palette lent the recordings a jazzier edge, while the producer also gave the album a more commercial, polished sound. However it, too, failed to register upon release.

BEEN SMOKING TOO LONG

Slipping into a depressive funk, Drake began to isolate himself at home, smoking copious amounts of marijuana. His record label, Island, tried to encourage him to make more live appearances and undertake interviews to promote the album, while family members urged the singer to visit a psychiatrist, resulting in him undertaking a course of antidepressants.

Under these circumstances, Drake recorded his final album, *Pink Moon*, in just two two-hour sessions in the early hours during October 1971. Defiantly anti-commercial, this time around Drake's music featured no backing, just his own accompaniment on guitar, with piano overdubs on the title track. Downbeat and introspective, the likes of 'Parasite', 'Which Will' and 'Things Behind The Sun' reveal the singer's dark state of mind at the time. When it was released in February 1972, the album fared even less well than its predecessors.

That same year, Drake suffered a nervous breakdown, essentially disappearing for a couple of years. In 1974, the singer emerged with plans to record a new album, though attempted sessions were problematic. Still taking antidepressants, Drake overdosed at his parents' home in November that year, after ingesting the antidepressant amitriptyline. In the ensuing decades, the singer's work has been reassessed, his three albums now hailed as classic singer-songwriter recordings. Drake, however, did not live to see the acclaim he longed for.

DATE OF BIRTH
19 June 1948
DATE OF DEATH
25 November 1974
GENRES
Folk, folk-rock

ONLY THE
GOOD DIE YOUNG

EAZY-E
BOY-N-THE-HOOD

'A brother that'll smother ya mother/And make ya sister think I love her.' So Eazy-E introduces himself on N.W.A's 1988 single 'Straight Outta Compton'. A high school dropout who took to selling drugs, Eric Wright had *bona fide* experience in street crime before turning to hip-hop and introducing the world to 'gangsta rap'.

Having made thousands of dollars from dealing marijuana, Eazy caught hip-hop's rising tide in the late 1980s, launching the Ruthless record label during the music's 'golden age'. With rapper Ice Cube and rapper/producer Dr Dre, Eazy formed Niggaz Wit Attitudes, releasing the *N.W.A And The Posse* collection in 1987. Settling around a five-man crew including MC Ren and DJ Yella, their first album kicked the doors open for 'gangsta rap' to burst through.

PARENTAL DISCRETION IZ ADVISED

With its explicit lyrics recounting tales of street violence, drug abuse and sexual escapades, *Straight Outta Compton* was instantly surrounded by controversy, not least for attracting the FBI's interest over its second track, 'Fuck Tha Police'. Though it attained instant infamy, the album also introduced a worldwide audience to the real-life struggles that black youths faced in this notoriously violent Los Angeles suburb. Around the same time, Eazy released a solo album, *Eazy-Duz-It*, mining the same material but without the same impact.

Feeling he was owed more money for having written much of *Straight Outta Compton*'s lyrics, Ice Cube left the group. On their 1990 EP *100 Miles And Runnin'*, and the following year's *Niggaz4Life* album, N.W.A started a public battle.

ONLY THE
GOOD DIE YOUNG

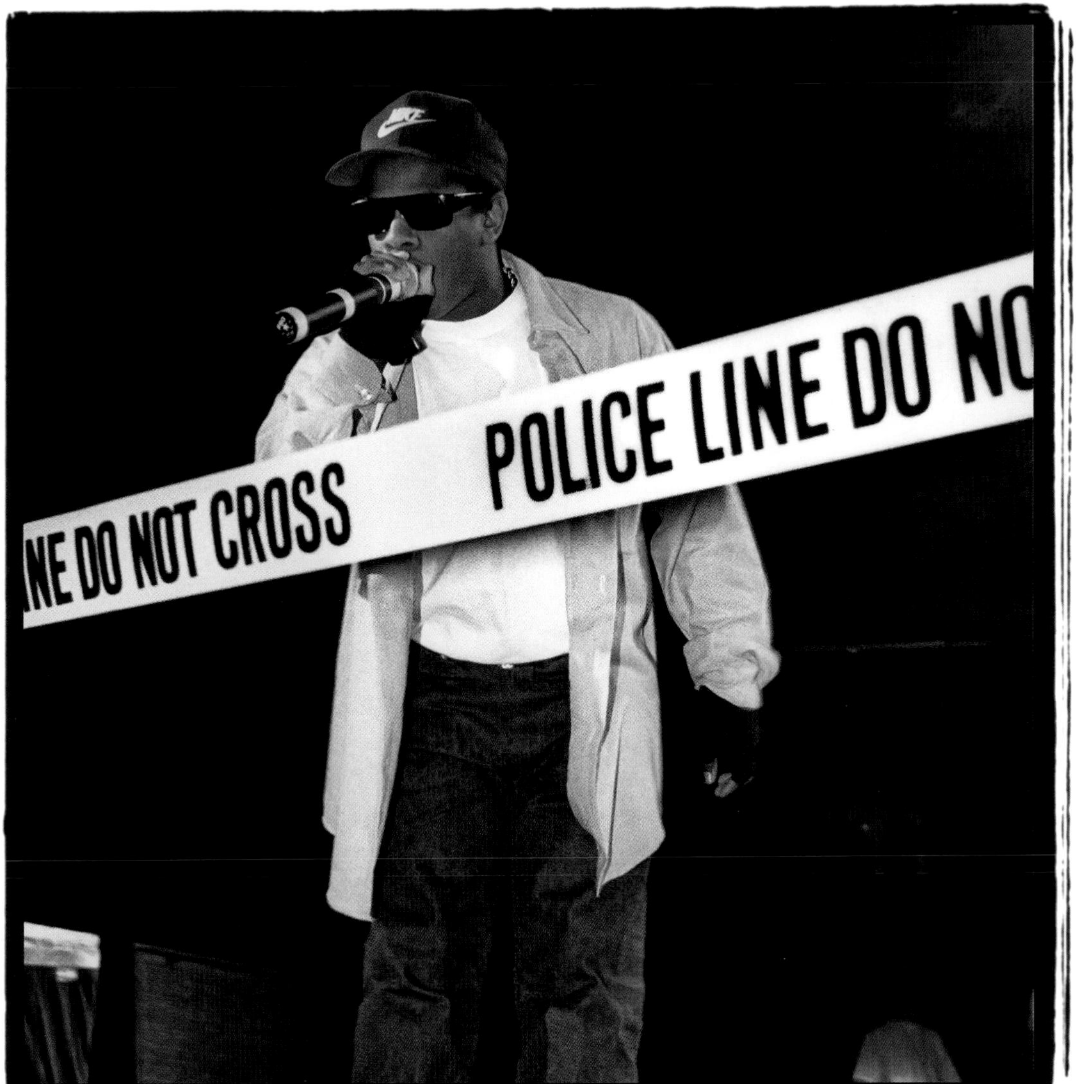
NIKE
POLICE LINE DO NO
NE DO NOT CROSS

criticizing their former member and questioning his authenticity, particularly on the track 'Real Niggaz'. In response, Cube closed his second solo album, *Death Certificate*, with 'No Vaseline', upping the ante on N.W.A and taking shots at their new manager.

2 HARD MUTHAS

But Ice Cube might have been on to something. With Jerry Heller now managing the group, Dr Dre began to feel as though Eazy-E was getting all the glory – and money – while the rest of N.W.A were being overlooked. Dre teamed up with Suge Knight, the physically imposing co-founder of the rival Death Row imprint, seeking to extricate himself from the Ruthless contract. When he finally did so, N.W.A disbanded.

An even longer-standing public rivalry played out between Dre and Eazy, both on record and in promotional videos. Yet while Eazy-E went on to release the *5150: Home 4 Tha Sick* and pointedly titled *It's On (Dr Dre) 187um Killa* EPs in 1992 and 1993 respectively – the latter topping the R&B/hip-hop chart while also peaking at No. 5 on the Top 200 – Dre's debut album, *The Chronic*, eclipsed all in its wake, going on to be hailed as a defining work in West Coast hip-hop.

Believing he had asthma, Eazy checked himself into Los Angeles' Cedars-Sinai Medical Center in February 1995, but received the shock diagnosis of AIDS. Eazy died from the disease just a month later, having pioneered a hip-hop style that continues to draw on the headline-grabbing shock tactics he pioneered with N.W.A.

DATE OF BIRTH

7 September 1963

DATE OF DEATH

26 March 1995

GENRES

Hip-hop

RICHEY EDWARDS

BORN TO END

Though achieving their biggest commercial success with 1996's No. 2 album *Everything Must Go* and 1998's chart-topping *This Is My Truth Tell Me Yours*, The Manic Street Preachers' most enduring work was recorded in the early-to-mid-1990s, when the three-piece traded as a four-piece.

Richey Edwards joined the Welsh group as guitarist and lyricist, following the release of their debut single, 1988's 'Suicide Alley'. The resulting *New Art Riot* EP, released in 1990, and the following year's 'Motown Junk' single set out the group's stall: iconoclastic manifestos tied together with glam-tinged punk music and Edwards' knack for writing lyrics that fit perfectly with the 1990s' end-of-millennium tension. While promoting the group's 1991 single 'You Love Us', *NME* journalist and future BBC radio presenter Steve Lamacq challenged Edwards as to the group's sincerity. Edwards' infamous response was to carve '4 REAL' into his arm with a razor. The injury needed 18 stitches.

ARCHIVES OF PAIN

Bursting with politically charged lyrics, The Manics' first album, *Generation Terrorists*, came out the following year. The group had not yet settled into themselves though, and the following year's *Gold Against The Soul* remains an idiosyncratic release. Less political than its predecessor, it also saw The Manics try to write more commercial material, sitting at odds with their own artistic instincts.

Edwards was further conflicted and often admitted to self-harming. Drug and alcohol abuses, coupled with anorexia and depression, added to an increasingly desperate state. Edwards focused intently on writing lyrics for the group's

ONLY THE
GOOD DIE YOUNG

third album, resulting in a work by turns baffling, terrifying, devastating and moving. Yet Edwards' very personal vision was not entirely alienating; mixed with the group's return to aggressive, post–punk influences, *The Holy Bible* peaked at No. 6 in the charts when it was released in 1994.

FROM DESPAIR TO WHERE

Edwards checked into the Priory clinic following the album's release, though The Manics appeared on *Top Of The Pops* as a four–piece, earning them the honour of receiving the most complaints for a BBC broadcast at that time. The full band toured in support of the album, Edwards making his final appearance with them in December 1994.

On 1 February 1995, The Manics were due to travel to America for a tour. Edwards checked out of his London hotel that morning, however, and drove back home to Cardiff, Wales. In the weeks that followed, the guitarist was reportedly sighted several times around Newport, and had been removing large sums of money from his bank account on a daily basis. On 17 February his car was reported as having been abandoned at the Severn View service station.

Edwards has not been officially sighted since. Rumours of his whereabouts have been persistent, but never founded, while the widely accepted explanation is that the musician committed suicide by jumping off the Severn Bridge. In November 2008 he was officially 'presumed dead'. Now one of the biggest bands in the world, The Manic Street Preachers continue in their original three–piece line–up, while their 2009 album, *Journal For Plague Lovers*, found them reinvigorated with recordings of Edwards' previously unused lyrics.

DATE OF BIRTH

22 December 1967

DATE OF DEATH

23 November 2008 (presumed)

GENRES

Alternative rock

'MAMA' CASS ELLIOT

CALIFORNIA DREAMER

Ellen Naomi Cohen was dubbed the Earth Mother Of Hippiedom during America's late 1960s counter-cultural revolution. While The Mamas & The Papas would never seem as hip as their West Coast contemporaries such as Jefferson Airplane or The Doors, 'Mama' Cass Elliot (pictured second from the left) helped give them credibility, thanks to an early career that included work with the likes of future Lovin' Spoonful co-founder Zal Yanovsky.

After her Mugwumps bandmate Denny Doherty left to join husband-and-wife team John and Michelle Phillips in The New Journeymen, Cass was invited to make the trio a foursome, renaming themselves The Mamas & The Papas. A string of era-defining folk-rock hits followed, until the group released their final album, *People Like Us*, in 1971. By then a major force in her own right (she had already fronted a TV special and released a solo album, 1968's *Dream A Little Dream*) Cass struck out on her own. Her fifth LP, *Don't Call Me Mama Anymore*, came out in 1973. During a two-week sell-out engagement at the London Palladium the following year, Cass suffered a fatal heart attack in her hotel room.

DATE OF BIRTH

19 September 1941

DATE OF DEATH

29 July 1974

GENRES

Folk-rock, psychedelic rock, pop

ONLY THE GOOD DIE YOUNG

PETE FARNDON

PRETENDERS' SAFE BASS

After moving to London in 1973 and working on music paper *NME*, Chrissie Hynde became a regular on the punk circuit. Recording some demos of her own, she was encouraged to form a band and held auditions for what would become The Pretenders.

Bassist Pete Farndon – known for his flashy designer instruments – was the first recruited, and was quickly joined by guitarist James Honeyman–Scott and, eventually, drummer Martin Chambers. Despite the promise of Hynde's own material, the group's first single was a cover of The Kinks' 'Stop Your Sobbing', produced by new–wave artist Nick Lowe. Sex Pistols producer Chris Thomas was behind the decks for the critically and commercially acclaimed No. 1 album *Pretenders*, released in 1980 and featuring the group's biggest hit, 'Brass In Pocket'.

Pretenders II almost recaptured the magic the following year, peaking at No. 7, though Farndon's own fortunes were in decline. His drug habit resulted in the group sacking the bassist in 1982. In April the following year, Farndon became the second original Pretenders member (after James Honeyman–Scott) to die, when he drowned in a bathtub after taking heroin.

DATE OF BIRTH

12 June 1952

DATE OF DEATH

14 April 1983

GENRES

Alternative rock

ONLY THE
GOOD DIE YOUNG

FREAKY TAH

GHETTO PRINCE

With single titles such as 1995's 'Lifestyles Of The Rich & Shameless' and 'Jeeps, Lex Coups, Bimaz & Benz', Lost Boyz's first two releases introduced the hip-hop four-piece as a crew with their mind on their money and their money on their mind. Their third single, 1996's 'Renee', revealed a different side to the group. Lamenting the fatal shooting of a 'ghetto princess', it was released on the soundtrack for spoof gangsta rap film, *Don't Be A Menace To South Central While Drinking Your Juice In The Hood*.

Though their singles hardly troubled the upper reaches of the charts, their 1996 and 1997 albums, *Legal Drug Money* and *Love, Peace & Nappiness* respectively, were Top 10 hits in the US. While recording their third LP, Lost Boyz MC Mr Cheeks threw a 28th birthday party in the Sheraton Hotel in Queens, New York City. While leaving the hotel, the group's hype man, Freaky Tah, was shot in the back of the head. His murderer, Kelvin Jones, pleaded guilty. The group split in 1999 after *LB IV Life*'s disappointing performance, though the surviving Boyz returned in 2010, releasing the single 'Haaay' online.

DATE OF BIRTH

14 May 1971

DATE OF DEATH

28 March 1999

GENRES

Hip-hop

ONLY THE
GOOD DIE YOUNG

BOBBY FULLER

DID THE LAW FIGHT HIM?

Enamoured with Buddy Holly and Elvis Presley, Bobby Fuller (pictured second from the left) learned guitar as a teenager in the late 1950s. He spent most of his early 1960s career recording in a homemade studio in El Paso, Texas, with his brother and an ever-changing group of musicians. Fuller honed his recording skills by hiring out his home studio to local bands that he could produce.

A regular performer on the El Paso club circuit, Fuller doggedly persisted with rock'n'roll's basic formula. In December 1965 The Bobby Fuller Four released a version of The Crickets' Sonny Curtis-penned 'I Fought The Law', which went on to enter the Top 10. Just a few months later, in July 1966, Fuller would be found dead in mysterious circumstances: his body was covered in petechial haemorrhages – signs of broken blood vessels – and soaked in petrol, the inhalation of which probably caused his death. Though first officially ruled a suicide (later revised to 'accidental asphyxiation'), more sinister rumours – including a botched police investigation and the involvement of mass murderer Charles Manson – have persisted in lieu of any conclusive evidence.

DATE OF BIRTH

22 October 1942

DATE OF DEATH

18 July 1966

GENRES

Rock, pop

ONLY THE
GOOD DIE YOUNG

STEVE GAINES

ED KING'S LOSS WAS SOUTHERN ROCK'S GAINES

Having formed in 1964, by the mid-1970s the Jacksonville, Florida-based Lynyrd Skynrd were well on the way to perfecting their populist blend of Southern boogie and blues-rock. Their first two albums had gone gold within 18 months of their release, while their third record, 1975's *Nuthin' Fancy*, entered the Top 10.

It took the addition of guitarist Steve Gaines to the six-piece for the band to reach their peak. Introduced to the group by his sister Cassie (employed as one of the backing vocalists The Honkettes), Steve's guitar-playing amazed frontman Ronnie Van Zant and he was invited to join the band on tour (Gaines' third show with the band created the recordings for the 1976 live album, *One From The Road*). He had the musical ability, but he also had the singing and songwriting skills, providing essential input to 1977's Top 5-charting *Street Survivors*. Just three days after the album's release, the band's plane ran out of fuel and Gaines, his sister Cassie and Van Zant all died in the crash.

DATE OF BIRTH

14 September 1949

DATE OF DEATH

20 October 1977

GENRES

Southern rock

ONLY THE
GOOD DIE YOUNG

STEPHEN GATELY

THE BOYS' OWN SINGER

In the early 1990s, the world was awash with boy bands looking to emulate the success of Take That. Pop impresario Louis Walsh set out to create an Irish answer to the Manchester five-piece in 1993 when he advertised auditions for a group in Dublin. After whittling the hundreds of applicants down, a five-piece was formed including Ronan Keating, Stephen Gately, Keith Duffy and Shane Lynch. Over the following 12 months, the remaining slot alternated as Boyzone failed to attract a record deal but, by the time of their first single, 1994's 'Working My Way Back To You', Mikey Graham had joined the group, solidifying the famous five-man line-up.

'Working My Way Back To You' hit No. 3 in the Irish charts, though failed to gain any traction elsewhere. With the backing of major label Polygram, a cover of The Osmonds' 'Love Me For A Reason' topped the Irish charts, while peaking at No. 2 in the UK and making dents in the European markets. *Said And Done*, released the same month, in November 1994, topped the charts in both Ireland and the UK.

WHERE WE BELONG

Though Boyzone rose in popularity with covers of Cat Stevens' 'Father And Son' in 1995 and The Bee Gees' 'Words' the following year, the group's own songwriting started to come into its own for 1996's *A Different Beat*. Again, the album topped the charts in the UK and Ireland, while the group-penned title track went to No. 1 in the UK (No. 2 in Ireland), and Ronan Keating helped steer 'Isn't It A Wonder' to No. 2 in the UK (again landing one position lower in the group's homeland).

ONLY THE
GOOD DIE YOUNG

By the time of third album *Where We Belong*, success seemed guaranteed. A No. 1 album in 1998, spawning five hits singles – three No. 2 releases and two chart-toppers – it included 'No Matter What', an Andrew Lloyd Webber/ Jim Steinman creation that became the group's best-selling single, and even attracted a cover from Meat Loaf, who recorded it for his 1998 collection *The Very Best Of*.

KEY TO MY LIFE

Having achieved such phenomenal success, Boyzone went on hiatus in 2000 while its individual members pursued solo projects. The previous year, Stephen Gately had come out as gay – one of the first mainstream popstars to do so. Boyzone fans – predominantly teenage girls – supported the singer, sending his first solo single, the double-A-sided 'New Beginning'/'Bright Eyes' to No. 3 in the charts the year that Boyzone split, while helping his *New Beginning* solo album to reach No. 9.

Compared to life with Boyzone, Gately spent much of the 2000s out of the public eye, making a few television and theatre appearances, and marrying boyfriend Andrew Coles in a civil partnership ceremony in 2006. Two years later, Boyzone reformed, releasing new singles and embarking on a sell-out tour. In 2009, however, Gately died suddenly of a heart defect while holidaying in Majorca with Coles. Boyzone's fourth album, 2010's *Brother*, featured Gately's final recordings and topped the charts in the UK and Ireland.

DATE OF BIRTH

17 March 1976

DATE OF DEATH

10 October 2009

GENRES

Pop

ONLY THE
GOOD DIE YOUNG

LOWELL GEORGE

FEAT OF STRENGTH

Whether sacked for writing a song about drugs ('Willin''), playing a 15-minute guitar solo with his amp off, or just being too good for The Mothers Of Invention, Frank Zappa's loss was rock's gain, as Lowell George left to form Little Feat. Zappa managed to get the group a contract, though, and in 1969, the four-piece embarked on an eclectic career that took in country-rock, jazz-rock and many points in between.

Their 1971 self-titled debut LP went down badly and Little Feat disbanded before a new line-up convened for the following year's *Sailin' Shoes*. 1973's *Dixie Chicken* and 1974's *Feats Don't Fail Me Now* saw the band on form and are exemplary blues-rock albums characterized by George's songwriting and playing. As the other band members pursued more esoteric, jazz-tinged routes, however, George took more of a back seat role as producer. While on tour following the release of his 1979 solo album, *Thanks, I'll Eat It Here*, the chronically overweight George collapsed and suffered a heart attack brought on by years of substance abuse. Little Feat continue to perform in various line-ups.

DATE OF BIRTH

13 April 1945

DATE OF DEATH

29 January 1979

GENRES

Blues-rock, rock'n'roll, Southern rock

ONLY THE
GOOD DIE YOUNG

ANDY GIBB

SHADOW DANCER

The youngest of the Gibb brothers (including Bee Gees' Barry, Maurice and Robin), Andy Gibb did not follow in his siblings' footsteps. While the Bee Gees started making a name for themselves in Australia, where the brothers grew up, Andy was travelling and performing with his own band, Melody Fayre.

With Bee Gees releases starting to gain worldwide attention in the late 1960s and early 1970s, Barry convinced his brother to return to Australia. In 1975, Andy released his first solo single 'Words And Music', which at least put him on the map, despite only being distributed within Australia and New Zealand.

A FAMILY AFFAIR

With eldest brother Barry at the controls, Andy entered the studio in 1976 to record a solo album. The May 1977 release of 'I Just Want To Be Your Lover' not only topped the charts in Australia, but also the US, paving the way for Andy's debut album, *Flowing Rivers*. Peaking at No. 19 in the States, its second single, '(Love Is) Thicker Than Water' even knocked his brothers' all-conquering 'Stayin' Alive' off *Billboard*'s Hot 100 top spot, only to be usurped by the Bee Gees' 'Night Fever' in February 1978.

With the Gibb brothers – either the solo performer or Bee Gees collective – dominating the charts, all four took to writing the title track of Andy's follow-up album, 1978's *Shadow Dancing*. The dream team collaboration made Andy the first male solo artist to release three consecutive chart-topping singles in the US, while the song's success helped push the LP to No. 7 in the US charts.

As the 1980s dawned, Andy's successes declined, and even the Bee Gees' prolific work rate slowed while each brother took to recording solo projects. When Andy's third album, *After Dark*, only just failed to enter the Top 20, he began looking towards acting as a parallel career. (The two disciplines entwined when he briefly dated *Dallas* actress Victoria Principal, releasing 'All I Have To Do Is Dream' as a duet with her; it stalled just outside the US Top 50.)

A CHANGE OF DIRECTION

With leading roles in both *Joseph And The Amazing Technicolor Dreamcoat* and *Pirates Of Penzance*, Gibb also co-hosted the second season of US pop TV show *Solid Gold* in the early 1980s. Having developed a habit of disappearing on long drug-fuelled weekends, however, his contracts were short-lived. Checking in to the Betty Ford Clinic in the mid-1980s, Gibb emerged to stage a greatest hits tour and take on minor roles in US TV shows.

As he approached 30, Gibb started working on new material with brothers Barry and Maurice, signing a record contract with the iconic Island record label. Yet five days after a party celebrating his birthday, Andy checked into Oxford's John Radcliffe Hospital, suffering chest pains. He died later that day from inflammation of the heart. In the 1990s, there was a renewal of interest in the Bee Gees. 2010's *Mythology* box set contained one of Andy's final works, the 1987 recording 'Arrow Through The Heart'.

DATE OF BIRTH

5 March 1958

DATE OF DEATH

10 March 1988

GENRES

Pop, disco

JOHN GLASCOCK

DANCING FANDANGOS IN HEAVEN

London–born bassist John Glascock (pictured on the far left) joined prog–rock group Carmen in 1973, after they relocated to London from Los Angeles. Three albums of flamenco–rock fusion followed (1973's *Fandangos In Space*, the following year's *Dancing On A Cold Wind* and 1975's *The Gypsies*), before Carmen split and Glascock joined Jethro Tull.

Tull were at a crossroads: having made their name with prog–rock concept albums such as 1971's *Aqualung* and the following year's *Thick As A Brick*, the Ian Anderson–led group's music was undergoing a sea change. Though Glascock would contribute to 1976's *Too Old To Rock'n'Roll: Too Young To Die!*, it would prove to be the band's final out–and–out prog–rock concept album, with Jethro Tull releasing a string of folk–rock–tinged recordings as the 1970s drew to a close. Glascock's death in 1979 – of a congenital heart defect for which he had received open heart surgery just a year before – brought the curtain down on Tull's most successful decade. The group has continued to record and perform across the decades, while Ian Anderson released his *Thick As A Brick 2* solo album in 2012.

DATE OF BIRTH

2 May 1951

DATE OF DEATH

17 November 1979

GENRES

Rock, blues–rock, prog–rock

CHARLES HADDON

GOLDEN YEARS CUT TRAGICALLY SHORT

In the electro-pop boom of the late 2000s, London synth trio Ou Est Le Swimming Pool were set to make waves. In just their first year of existence, the band made key UK festival appearances at Glastonbury and Bestival in 2009, while also supporting synth-pop media darling La Roux the following year. Their single releases – 2009's 'Dance The Way I Feel' and 'These New Knights', and the following year's 'Jackson's Last Stand' – began to build a steady following in anticipation of their debut LP, *The Golden Year*, but the album release was delayed following a tragedy at Belgium's Pukkelpop festival in August 2010.

After lead singer Charles Haddon performed a stage dive into the crowd during the band's performance, he became distraught, worrying that he'd injured a young girl in the audience. Such was his distress that Haddon committed suicide after the show by jumping from a telecommunications pole and into a car park behind the festival's main stage. When *The Golden Year* came out in October, it was preceded by a tribute festival, Chazzstock, held in Camden, where the band was based.

DATE OF BIRTH

1988

DATE OF DEATH

20 August 2010

GENRES

Pop, dance

LYNDEN DAVID HALL

UK SOUL'S BRIGHTEST STAR

UK soul is often considered an inferior cousin to its US counterpart. Lynden Hall helped raise its stature by becoming the first home-grown singer to be voted Best Male Artist by the UK-based *Blues & Soul* magazine – just one year after he received the Best Newcomer award at the 1998 MOBO ceremony. His debut album, 1997's eerily presciently titled *Medicine 4 My Pain*, charted at No. 43 and spawned four singles. The original recordings appealed to traditional soul fans, while remixes of his work played well in the charts. After being reissued in 1998, 'Sexy Cinderella' became Hall's biggest hit, reaching the Top 20.

Hall's 2000 album, *The Other Side*, built upon his success and peaked at No. 36. Such was the singer's stature that he was invited to perform in the British romcom *Love Actually*. A month before the film's release, Hall was diagnosed with Hodgkin's lymphoma, adding a poignancy to his on-screen performance of 'All You Need Is Love'. He released his final album, *In Between Jobs*, in April 2005, before succumbing to the disease seven months later, on Valentine's Day.

DATE OF BIRTH

7 May 1974

DATE OF DEATH

14 February 2006

GENRES

R&B, soul

PETER HAM

WITHOUT HIM

Signing to The Beatles' Apple imprint in 1968 as The Iveys (under which name they released their debut album, *Maybe Tomorrow*), Peter Ham's band began pointing in the right direction when they rechristened themselves Badfinger for 1970's *Magic Christian Music*. Inevitably compared to The Beatles – Ham had ingested all the Fabs' pop-rock influences – the group's best-known song, 'Come And Get It', with writing and production by Paul McCartney, reached No. 4 in the UK charts and No. 7 in the US.

Ham's greatest moment as a songwriter was to follow. Tucked away on their third LP, 1970's *No Dice*, 'Without You' became a worldwide smash on the back of Harry Nilsson's iconic cover in 1972. The Apple imprint's haphazard business model finally collapsed around Badfinger, however, and the group moved to major label Warner Bros in 1974 for their self-titled sixth album. Vastly declining chart success and internal band and managerial conflicts began to weigh heavily on Ham, who hanged himself in his garage in 1975. Various line-ups went on to tour from the late 1970s into the late 1980s.

DATE OF BIRTH

27 April 1947

DATE OF DEATH

24 April 1975

GENRES

Rock, pop-rock

LESLIE HARVEY

STONE COLD CLASSIC

The younger brother of theatrical Scottish rocker Alex Harvey, Leslie was no stranger to tragedy by the time he formed Stone The Crows with blues belter Maggie Bell in 1969. Having cut his teeth in his brother's Soul Band, Harvey released an LP, *Baby Don't Look Down*, in 1965 with The Blues Council, before an automobile accident killed half the group.

Supporting Led Zeppelin on a US tour in 1969, as part of the band Cartoone, Harvey met the headliner's tour manager Peter Grant. Later that year, Grant would rename Harvey's new Glasgow-based blues-rock five-piece Stone The Crows. With Maggie Bell up front, they were something of a Scottish answer to Janis Joplin's work with the likes of Big Brother & The Holding Company. They recorded four albums, their final LP, 1972's *Continuous Performance*, reaching No. 3 in the charts. On tour that year, Harvey had wet hands when he touched a microphone live on stage at Swansea's Top Rank venue. The equipment was not grounded, fatally electrocuting the guitarist.

DATE OF BIRTH

13 September 1944

DATE OF DEATH

3 May 1972

GENRES

Rock, blues

DONNY HATHAWAY
SOUL DUETTIST DESERVES HIS DUES

Like many great songwriters from soul's golden age, Donny Hathaway spent his apprentice years working as a session musician and songwriter. Learning his trade at Chicago's Twilight imprint in the late 1960s before moving to Curtis Mayfield's Curtom label, Hathaway released his first single in 1969, 'I Thank You Baby', as a duet with June Conquest.

Atlantic subsidiary Atco picked him up later that year, releasing *Everything Is Everything* LP in 1970. A No. 33 R&B hit, it kicked off an incredibly prolific period in which Hathaway co-wrote and recorded 'This Christmas'. In 1972 he scored his biggest commercial success with an LP of cover versions and original recordings with Roberta Flack, which peaked at No. 3 in the US pop charts. A string of soundtrack scores followed before he released *Extension Of A Man* in 1973. Debilitating bouts of depression threatened to derail the singer's career, and Hathaway didn't return to the charts until 1978's 'The Closer I Get To You', another R&B chart-topper with Roberta Flack. After a recording session in January 1979, Hathaway killed himself, taking a 15-storey leap from his hotel room balcony.

DATE OF BIRTH

1 October 1945

DATE OF DEATH

13 January 1979

GENRES

Soul, pop

HELNO

FRENCH REVOLUTIONARY

Nine-piece Les Négresses Vertes brought a DIY attitude to their ambitious vision of world music, taking in brass instruments and an accordionist, despite being a collection of friends who had barely touched any instruments. Mixing Latin, reggae, punk, raï and French folk music, the results were a sprawling collision of the band members' Spanish, Algerian, French and gypsy heritage.

Parisian lyricist and frontman Noël Rota (aka Helno Rota de Lourcqua) led the charge with the group's first single release, 1988's '200 Ans D'Hypocrisie': an aggressive challenge to his homeland's French Revolution celebrations. It was followed by debut album *Mlah*, which unleashed the group's full, freewheeling sound. Yet while the Négresses began gaining worldwide recognition, Helno was locked in a personal battle with heroin addiction. For 1991's follow-up album, *Famille Nombreuse*, guitarist Stefane Mellino took over songwriting duties with the aid of accordionist Matthias Canavese. Helno toured in support of the album, before moving in with his parents in an attempt to clean up. In January 1993, he died of an overdose. A downsized Les Négresses Vertes continued to record into the mid-2000s.

DATE OF BIRTH

25 December 1963

DATE OF DEATH

22 January 1993

GENRES

World, alternative rock

ONLY THE
GOOD DIE YOUNG

JIMI HENDRIX

STAR-SPANGLED SIX-STRINGER

One of the most innovative guitarists of the twentieth century, Hendrix not only revolutionized the way his instrument was played, but also used an array of effects pedals and studio tricks to conjure new sounds. From Eric Clapton teasing his own hair into an afro, to Eddie Hazel's Funkadelic explorations and Prince's fusion of funk and rock styles, Hendrix's legacy arguably looms larger than any other musician's.

If he hadn't been so lackadaisical when it came to rules, Hendrix might never have become a legend. As it was, the guitarist proved of little use to the US Army, which discharged him after a year of service. Decamping to Tennessee, Hendrix formed a band with fellow soldier and bassist Billy Cox, though soon tired of the local scene and moved to New York City. Work with The Isley Brothers, Little Richard and Curtis Knight quickly followed, though Hendrix was better suited as leader of his own band, fronting Jimmy James & The Blues Flames. In 1966, The Animals' ex-bassist, Chas Chandler, offered to be his manager, taking Hendrix to the UK, where his career flourished.

THE NEW RISING SUN

An immediate hit on the UK club scene, Hendrix formed The Jimi Hendrix Experience with bassist Noel Redding and drummer Mitch Mitchell. The three-piece's astonishing live performances were replicated on record for 1967's *Are You Experienced*, with Hendrix mastering blues, rock and psych music, fusing them into his own sound. The album reached No. 2 in the UK charts, just behind The Beatles' *Sgt Pepper's Lonely Hearts Club Band*.

ONLY THE
GOOD DIE YOUNG

Returning to the States, Hendrix performed a breakout show at the Monterey Pop Festival. Forever enshrined as the musician who set his guitar on fire – as he did that night – the guitarist's incendiary performance ensured that he also burnt his bridges with the past, pointing the way towards the future of guitar-based rock'n'roll.

Though hailed as a live performer, Hendrix preferred recording in the studio. Released at the tail end of 1967, *Axis: Bold As Love* built upon what had gone before, the guitarist layering his music in ever more complex effects. Over the next 12 months, Hendrix obsessed over multiple takes of recordings, expanding his sound way beyond the trio's live capabilities, resulting in *Electric Ladyland*. Containing some of his most famous recordings, including 'Voodoo Child (Slight Return)', the album became his only US chart-topper.

KiSS THE SKY

Disbanding the Experience (though retaining Mitchell on drums), Hendrix spent much of 1969 and 1970 in flux. Flanked by various musicians – including reuniting with bassist Billy Cox – he made a career-defining appearance at the 1969 Woodstock Festival. Work on a fourth album, *First Rays Of The New Rising Sun*, continued into 1970, while Hendrix set out on a European tour in autumn. Having spent the night of 17 September partying, he died in the early hours of the following morning, choking on his own vomit after mixing sleeping pills with red wine. Hendrix continues to influence every guitarist who follows in his wake, while a seemingly endless amount of live and studio recordings has surfaced as both official and unofficial posthumous releases.

DATE OF BiRTH

27 November 1942

DATE OF DEATH

18 September 1970

GENRES

Psychedelic rock, hard rock, blues-rock

ONLY THE
GOOD DiE YOUNG

BUDDY HOLLY

PIONEERING ROCK'N'ROLL SONGWRITER

While a teenager in Lubbock, Texas, Holly and school friend Bob Montgomery performed as a country music duo. After playing on the same bill as Elvis Presley in 1955, Holly incorporated the rhythmic drive of Presley's music into his own, creating a proto-rockabilly hybrid of country and rock'n'roll music. A further support slot for Bill Haley cemented the nascent songwriter's move towards the new music craze sweeping the nation, while gaining him a recording contract with the Decca imprint.

With his new band The Crickets (guitarist Nikki Sullivan, bassist Joe B. Maudlin and drummer Jerry Allison), Holly entered the studio with future Nashville Sound architect Owen Bradley. The resulting recordings, including an early take on Holly's classic 'That'll Be The Day', were a disappointment. Single releases 'Blue Days, Black Nights' and 'Modern Don Juan' failed to enter the charts and Decca dropped Holly in January 1957.

RAVE ON

Signing himself to Coral and The Crickets to Brunswick – both Decca subsidiaries – Holly re-recorded 'That'll Be The Day' and released it under The Crickets' name. Doing so cleverly avoided legal claims from Decca that 'Buddy Holly' could not release the songs that he had recorded for the label.

Released in May 1957, the re-recorded 'That'll Be The Day' hit No. 1 in the US Hot 100, peaking at No. 2 in the R&B charts. In the strange position of having two recording contracts, Holly also released The "Chirping" Crickets later that year, while putting out his own self-titled LP in February 1958, the former featuring Top 10 hit 'Oh, Boy!' and the latter containing the No. 3 release 'Peggy Sue'.

ONLY THE
GOOD DIE YOUNG

Visits to the *Ed Sullivan Show* studios in New York further acquainted Holly with the machinations of the music industry, and the songwriter became increasingly interested in the publishing side of the business. Meeting future wife Maria Elena Santiago – a receptionist at the Peer–Southern Music publishers – furthered his involvement with the industry. When The Crickets returned home to Lubbock, Holly remained in the city, soaking up new musical influences and engrossing himself in the music business.

THE DAY THE MUSIC DIED

Having learned that his manager, Norman Petty, was banking the band's royalties himself, Holly began legal proceedings against him. With little money for himself, however, the singer assembled a new backing band, touring as part of the Winter Dance Party with Ritchie Valens, Dion & The Belmonts and The Big Bopper. Tired of travelling by bus, Holly, Valens and The Big Bopper opted to take a flight to one engagement; a piloting error, along with snowfall, caused the plane to crash, killing the musicians and their pilot.

Despite releasing music for little more than 18 months, Buddy's Holly's influence as one of rock'n'roll's first songwriters has lasted far beyond his lifetime. The Beatles, The Rolling Stones and Bob Dylan all took inspiration from Holly's work for their own pioneering recordings, while Don McLean would forever enshrine Holly's memory in song, lamenting his death as 'the day the music died' in his No. 1 US hit 'American Pie'.

DATE OF BIRTH

7 September 1936

DATE OF DEATH

3 February 1959

GENRES

Rock'n'roll

ONLY THE
GOOD DIE YOUNG

JAMES HONEYMAN-SCOTT

THE GREAT PRETENDER

Despite only appearing on The Pretenders' first two albums, James Honeyman-Scott's guitar style marked him out as one of the most innovative guitarists of the post-punk new wave. Fusing various British styles, from 1960s blues-rockers Cream to 1970s glam rockers Mott The Hoople and late-1970s/early-1980s new-wave firebrand Elvis Costello, Honeyman-Scott also looked to the US, incorporating influence from one-time Neil Young sideman Nils Lofgren and 1970s Southern-rockers The Allman Brothers. Such omnivorous tastes in music gave The Pretenders' recordings a transatlantic appeal that not only sold well in the UK, but also achieved success in frontwoman Chrissie Hynde's North American homeland.

Relocating from Ohio to London, Hynde found work on the UK's leading music weekly, the *NME*, before immersing herself in the city's emerging punk scene. A non-starting project with future Clash guitarist Mick Jones gave way to a brief stint with the group that would become The Damned. Having also been working on her own material, Hynde started looking for a band she could record it with.

TALK OF THE TOWN

Honeyman-Scott had known future Pretenders bassist Pete Farndon since the mid-1970s, and the latter recruited the guitarist for Hynde's rehearsals in 1978. Immediately hitting it off with the singer, Honeyman-Scott became an official member of the group. Before long, he was helping Hynde write the music to her songs, adding melodic lines to her rhythm guitar foundations, smoothing the punkier edges into something more radio-friendly. Hynde would later credit the guitarist with being the group's 'sound'.

ONLY THE
GOOD DIE YOUNG

One of Honeyman-Scott's influences, Nick Lowe, produced The Pretenders' first single, a cover of The Kinks' 'Stop Your Sobbing'. Edging to No. 34 in the UK, it paved the way for the No. 1 success of the group's self-titled 1980 debut album, produced by one-time Beatles engineer and Sex Pistols producer Chris Thomas. Further consolidating the group's success, the album's third single, 'Brass In Pocket', topped the UK charts while peaking at No. 14 in the US.

BAD BOYS GET SPANKED

Covering much the same ground – down to the inclusion of a Kinks cover, and eventual Top 10 single, 'I Go To Sleep' – *Pretenders II* came out in August 1981. Though failing to achieve the critical and commercial success of its predecessor, the album entered the Top 10 on both sides of the Atlantic, the final time the original line-up of the group would do so.

As the group rose to fame, drug use began to take hold over its members – notably Honeyman-Scott and Pete Farndon. A large tour supporting *Pretenders II* put strain on the group, particularly as Farndon grew more irascible, making it difficult for the band to work with him. Looking for a break, Honeyman-Scott retreated to Texas with his wife, only to be summoned back to London for a band meeting, during which Farndon was formally sacked. Two days later, Honeyman-Scott died of heart failure brought on by his cocaine use. Ten months later, Farndon would be the second Pretender to die a drug-related death.

DATE OF BIRTH

4 November 1956

DATE OF DEATH

16 June 1982

GENRES

Alternative rock

SHANNON HOON

FRUITFUL CAREER

After playing in local bands, Indiana native Richard Shannon Hoon relocated to Los Angeles in the late 1980s, where he met the musicians that would make up Blind Melon. Briefly taken under the aegis of Axl Rose, Hoon's career was given a boost with vocal spots on Guns N' Roses' *Use Your Illusion* albums. Blind Melon were subsequently invited to tour with the band in support of their self-titled debut, which hit No. 3 in the US charts.

Two years of heavy touring was matched by two years of heavy cocaine use. Hoon and his girlfriend became parents in the summer of 1995, coinciding with the release of Blind Melon's second album, *Soup*. Touring for that album elicited further drug use and, after a concert in Houston, on 20 October 1995, Hoon disappeared into a blizzard of cocaine, overdosing on the tour bus. The final Blind Melon album to feature him, *Nico* – named for his daughter – came out in 1996. The remainder of the band reconvened with a new singer for 2008's *For My Friends*.

DATE OF BIRTH

26 September 1967

DATE OF DEATH

21 October 1995

GENRES

Alternative rock

ROBERT JOHNSON

THE DEVIL HAS THE BEST TUNES

When it comes to rock'n'roll myths, 1930s Delta blues pioneer Robert Johnson wrote the book. The idea that he sold his soul to the Devil in return for the ability to play the blues has inspired countless songs, myths and wide-eyed awe from musicians throughout the decades. His discography – just 42 recordings made from 1936–37 – has influenced musicians from Bob Dylan and The Rolling Stones, though to Jack White in the early 2000s. That Johnson's biography can never be recounted with watertight factual accuracy only adds to the mystique; that his death is shrouded in as much mystery than his life just further fuels the legend.

Born in Mississippi in the early 1910s, Johnson lived with his father for a period, before returning to live with his mother in Mississippi. Aged 18 in 1929, he married a 16-year-old wife who, shortly after, died in childbirth. Despite fathering another child elsewhere, Johnson's second marriage would be to another woman whom he would leave in the early 1930s to pursue his career as a musician.

UP JUMPED THE DEVIL

Ten years Johnson's senior, Mississippi bluesman Son House came across Johnson, later recounting that he was an awful guitarist. Shortly after their encounter, Johnson disappeared – possibly searching for his biological father. When he returned, Johnson had mastered the instrument, playing slide blues, country and jazz music so advanced it sounded as though two people were playing simultaneously. This remarkable turnaround gave rise to the legend that Johnson had travelled to a Delta crossroads to meet the Devil, selling his soul in exchange for the ability to play revolutionary blues music.

ONLY THE
GOOD DIE YOUNG

In 1936 and 1937, Johnson attended a handful of recording sessions in Texas, laying down the songs for which he would become famous, among them 'Last Fair Deal Gone Down', 'Preaching Blues (Up Jumped The Devil)', 'Love In Vain', 'Stop Breaking Down Blues' and 'Terraplane Blues'. Though he would only live to see a mere quarter of his work released, the 42 songs captured – including second takes – formed the bedrock of modern blues and rock'n'roll music. The entire collection has been released throughout the ensuing decades.

LAST FAIR DEAL GONE DOWN

Accounts differ as to what exactly happened the night Johnson died, though the date has been pinned to 16 August 1938. Having spent much of the 1930s as a travelling bluesman throughout the South, Johnson's latest residency was just outside of Greenwood, Mississippi, providing entertainment at a country dance for several weeks. Some reports say that Johnson had flirted with the club owner's wife, whose husband subsequently poisoned the whisky bottle he was drinking from. Other stories claim that a different jealous husband was seeking revenge. The whisky is said to have been spiked with strychnine, which slowly killed the musician over three days, though even the type of poison has been the subject of much discussion. The uncertainty surrounding much of Johnson's life continues: several burial grounds have been identified as possible final resting places.

DATE OF BIRTH

8 May 1911

DATE OF DEATH

16 August 1938

GENRES

Delta blues, folk blues

ONLY THE
GOOD DIE YOUNG

BRIAN JONES
MIDNIGHT RAMBLER

With pin-up good looks and a flamboyant dress sense, Brian Jones was destined to stand out from the crowd. Even in Mick Jagger and Keith Richards' company, Jones could lay claim to inspiring manager Andrew Loog Oldham's inflammatory headline: 'Would You Let Your Daughter Marry A Rolling Stone?' Yet the founding band member is also its most tragic figure. Once their *de facto* leader – forming the group, naming them and getting them early gigs – he became increasingly marginalized as Jagger and Richards rose to prominence as songwriters.

Leaving home after getting his teenage girlfriend pregnant, Jones spent time in the late 1950s travelling Europe as a street performer, playing the blues music that he loved. In the early 1960s – and a father for the third time – he drifted into London, becoming a fixture on the local blues scene and performing as Elmo Lewis (a mixture of bluesman Elmore James' first name and Jones' own birth name). In 1962, Jones held auditions for a new R&B group, hiring pianist Ian Stewart, singer Mick Jagger and guitarist Keith Richards. Bassist Bill Wyman and drummer Charlie Watts completed the line-up, christened The Rolling Stones.

HAVE YOU SEEN YOUR FOUNDER, BABY, STANDING IN THE SHADOW?

Within two years, the Stones had released their first UK Top 5 single, 'Not Fade Away', and their self-titled No. 1 debut LP. Five No. 1 hits followed, including blues covers ('Little Red Rooster') and Jagger-Richards originals ('(I Can't Get No) Satisfaction', 'Get Off Of My Cloud'). By the mid-1960s, The Rolling Stones vied with The Beatles to be crowned hottest group in the British Invasion. As Jagger and Richards penned hit after hit, Jones broadened his own influence within

ONLY THE
GOOD DIE YOUNG

the group, notably expanding their sound with Middle Eastern sitar on the 1966 No. 1 hit 'Paint It, Black'. On the following year's decidedly psychedelic LP *Their Satanic Majesties Request*, Jones abandoned the guitar entirely, favouring the Mellotron, flute, electric dulcimer and saxophone.

Yet while Jones increased the Stones' musical palette he became distanced from Jagger and Richards, and his feelings of isolation drew him into progressively debilitating drug use. By 1968, Jones' contributions to the likes of 'Sympathy For The Devil' were being mixed out of recordings. The following year, he appeared on just two Rolling Stones songs.

YOU CAN'T ALWAYS GET WHAT YOU WANT

Rather than push the Stones forward, as he once had, Jones' erratic behaviour had started holding them back. In 1969, a planned US winter tour was in jeopardy, as two drug busts prohibited Jones from entering the country. In June that year, the musicians he had picked to form The Rolling Stones told Jones that they no longer needed his services.

Less than a month later, Jones' girlfriend, Anna Wohlin, found the ex-Stone drowned in his swimming pool at his Cotchford Farm home in Sussex. 'Death by misadventure' was the official cause. Rumours that the guitarist was murdered have persisted throughout the decades, most notably with claims that he was killed by Frank Thorogood, a builder working on Cotchford Farm at the time.

DATE OF BIRTH

28 February 1942

DATE OF DEATH

3 July 1969

GENRES

Rock, blues-rock, R&B

ONLY THE
GOOD DIE YOUNG

LINDA JONES

FORGOTTEN SOUL DIVA

Linda Jones was born in Newark, New Jersey, and was already performing in her family's gospel group, the Jones Singers, at the age of six. Her first recording, 'Lonely Teardrops' (under the name Linda Lane) was released on Cub Records in 1963, but her subsequent recordings for Atco Records and Blue Cat failed to break through. It was 'Hypnotized', recorded for Loma records (a subsidiary of Warner Bros) that proved to be her biggest hit, reaching No. 4 in the *Billboard* R&B charts in 1967, with the album of the same name from which it was taken also charting well.

It was on her later recordings for Turbo, however, that she fully developed her own distinctive style, raw and emotional, steeped in gospel as well as soul. Her 1972 cover of The Impressions' song, 'For Your Precious Love', provided her with her biggest hit since 'Hypnotized'. During a week-long residency at New York's Apollo Theatre she passed away from complications arising from diabetes whilst resting at home between afternoon and evening shows.

DATE OF BIRTH

14 December 1944

DATE OF DEATH

14 March 1972

GENRES

Soul

ONLY THE
GOOD DIE YOUNG

JANIS JOPLIN

THE QUEEN OF ROCK'N'ROLL

Owner of one of the most powerful female voices in the history of rock music, Janis Joplin was fascinated with the blues from an early age. She was introduced to the records of Lead Belly by a fellow student and was soon listening to such singers as Bessie Smith and Big Mama Thornton. One of the few white female singers of the time who could match the power of such figures, her raw delivery and ballsy stage persona masked a shy and sensitive personality.

Joplin was born in Port Arthur, Texas, but she did not have a happy time there during her adolescence. She moved briefly to Los Angeles in the summer of 1961, but returned to Port Arthur, leaving again for the University of Texas at Austin in 1962. There she began performing at folk clubs with the Waller Club Boys. In early 1963, she quit college and moved to San Francisco. This early attempt to break into the music business, however, was not a success.

BIG BROTHER & THE HOLDING COMPANY

Joplin's drinking and drug use had already proved problematic during her first stint in San Francisco, and she returned to Port Arthur in 1965, where she enrolled at Lamar University, continuing to commute to Austin to perform solo, backing herself up on guitar. But she was persuaded to return to San Francisco in 1966 to audition for Big Brother & The Holding Company, a psychedelic rock band who already had a local following. With Joplin at the helm, the band grew ever more popular, and their appearance at the 1967 Monterey Pop Festival brought them acclaim further afield, with Joplin delivering a stunning performance, especially on their version of the Big Mama Thornton song 'Ball and Chain'.

Their debut album, *Big Brother And The Holding Company* (1967), was released on Columbia shortly after their Monterey appearance. *Live At Winterland '68* captures performances in San Francisco in April 1968. *Cheap Thrills* (1968) went to No. 1, and produced hit singles with 'Piece of My Heart' and 'Summertime'. Joplin's increasingly prominent position in the line-up led to tensions within the band, and at the beginning of September 1968, feeling that the band was holding her back, Joplin announced she was quitting.

SOLO CAREER

The first band that Joplin formed on leaving Big Brother was The Kozmic Blues Band, releasing *I Got Dem Ol' Kozmic Blues Again Mama!* in 1969. They performed at Woodstock, but by the end of the year The Kozmic Blues Band had broken up.

She began touring with the Full Tilt Boogie Band in May 1970, with many critics rating this as her best backing band. But her appearance with them in Boston on 12 August was to be her last public performance. In late August the band began rehearsing and recording for their new album, the posthumously released *Pearl* (1971), which became the biggest selling of her career. But she was found dead in her room at the Landmark Motor Hotel on 4 October 1970, having overdosed on heroin.

DATE OF BIRTH

19 January 1943

DATE OF DEATH

4 October 1970

GENRES

Psychedelic rock

ONLY THE
GOOD DIE YOUNG

TERRY KATH

FOUNDER MEMBER OF ROCK GROUP CHICAGO

Multi-instrumentalist Terry Kath was born in Chicago, Illinois, and spent the mid- to late-1960s playing with a variety of bands including Jimmy & The Gentlemen and The Missing Links. Moving to Los Angeles with The Big Thing, he and the group were signed by Columbia Records and renamed Chicago Transit Authority, shortened in 1970 to Chicago.

Kath was a vital contributor to Chicago's recorded output up to 1977's *Chicago XI*, but it is 1969's *The Chicago Transit Authority* that perhaps contains his most innovative work, including his own composition 'Introduction' (described by later Chicago guitarist Dawayne Bailey as 'Terry's masterpiece'), and the instrumental 'Free Form Guitar', recorded live in the studio on a Stratocaster with a broken neck held together by a radiator hose clamp.

Known for his use of alcohol and drugs, Kath died after a party in Los Angeles in early 1978 whilst playing with a 9mm automatic pistol. After showing the empty magazine and saying 'Don't worry, it isn't loaded', he put the gun to his temple and pulled the trigger. He died instantly.

DATE OF BIRTH

31 January 1946

DATE OF DEATH

23 January 1978

GENRES

Rock, soft rock

ONLY THE
GOOD DIE YOUNG

PAUL KOSSOFF

FEARSOME ELECTRIC BLUES GUITARIST

There must have been something in the water in England in the mid–1960s, for that period saw the rise of an extremely talented and mostly extremely young crop of electric blues guitarists, including Eric Clapton, Jeff Beck, Peter Green, Jimmy Page and Paul Kossoff. Kossoff is in no way disgraced in such exalted company, and his skilful guitar work helped to make Free one of the most exciting bands of the early 1970s.

Kossoff was born in London in 1950, son of the actor David Kossoff. Although he studied classical guitar when he was younger, he had more or less stopped playing by his teenage years. But seeing Clapton play with John Mayall's Bluesbreakers in the winter of 1965 inspired him to take up the electric guitar and learn to play the blues.

EARLY YEARS

Kossoff joined Black Cat Bones in 1967, and the band became regulars on the London circuit, supporting Fleetwood Mac amongst others and playing with the touring American blues pianist Champion Jack Dupree. Kossoff and drummer Simon Kirke played on Dupree's 1968 album, *When You Feel The Feeling You Was Feeling*.

But it was when Kossoff and Kirke met vocalist Paul Rodgers in 1968 that something clicked, and with the addition of Andy Fraser on bass, Free was born. Playing incessantly in small clubs up and down the country, their debut, *Tons Of Sobs* (1968) was well received, as was *Free* (1969), and they built a loyal and dedicated following. But the single 'Broad Daylight' failed to take off, and Kossoff auditioned (unsuccessfully) for The Rolling Stones and Jethro Tull, who were both looking for new guitarists at that time.

ONLY THE
GOOD DIE YOUNG

The band's third album, *Fire And Water* (1970), proved to be their breakthrough success, propelled by the single 'All Right Now'. The band were now riding high, and an appearance at the Isle of Wight festival in the summer of that year cemented their reputation. After *Highway* (1970) was released, the band split, with Kossoff teaming up with keyboard player John 'Rabbit' Bundrick and bass player Tetsu Yamauchi for the 1971 album *Kossoff, Kirke, Tetsu And Rabbit*.

THE WRITING WAS ON THE WALL

Free reformed for *Free At Last* (1972) and *Heartbreaker* (1973). But the writing was on the wall. Fraser had left before the final album due to Kossoff's drug dependency (being replaced on *Heartbreaker* by Yamauchi), and Kossoff's own input on the final album was minimal. Kossoff was replaced by Wendell Richardson for the final tour, after which the band broke up for good. Kossoff released the solo *Back Street Crawler* (1973), which contained contributions from his former Free bandmates and Yes drummer Alan White, before forming the band of the same name in 1975, releasing two albums, *The Band Plays On* (1975) and *2nd Street* (1976). But Kossoff's health was worsening, and a spell in rehab in London in 1975 did not prevent him from continuing to use drugs. He died of a drug-induced heart attack while on a plane from Los Angeles to New York on 19 March 1976.

DATE OF BIRTH

14 September 1950

DATE OF DEATH

19 March 1976

GENRES

Blues rock, hard rock

ONLY THE
GOOD DIE YOUNG

SCOTT LA ROCK

PIONEERING HIP-HOP DJ

Born in Queens, Scott 'La Rock' Sterling (pictured on the right) moved with his mother at an early age to the Bronx. Although DJing regularly at the Broadway Repertoire Theatre by 1985, it was through his day job as a social worker at a homeless shelter that Sterling met KRS-One. The pair began recording together in the autumn of 1985, and eventually signed an agreement with Rock Candy Records and Filmworks to run a subsidiary label, B Boy Records, releasing their music under the name Boogie Down Productions (BDP).

Recorded in two hours, 'South Bronx' was the brilliant opening salvo in a lyrical war between Boogie Down Productions and Juice Crew, but it was BDP's 1987 debut album, *Criminally Minded*, with its inventive use of samples, taut drum programming and unflinching social commentary, that changed rap for ever.

Sterling and KRS were in the middle of negotiations with Warner Bros and had already begun pre-production on tracks that became the posthumously released *By All Means Necessary* (1988) when Sterling was wounded in a shooting incident in the Bronx on 26 August and died in hospital the next day.

DATE OF BIRTH

2 March 1962

DATE OF DEATH

27 August 1987

GENRES

Hip-hop

PETER LAUGHNER

UNDERGROUND AMERICAN GUITARIST

Described by writer Greil Marcus as 'the mad fool of the Cleveland punk movement', Peter Laughner (pictured on the right) had an immense influence over the Cleveland underground scene of the mid-1970s. He was born in Bay Village, Ohio, and was involved in a large variety of groups in Cleveland, including most notably Rocket From The Tombs and the early Pere Ubu. He also wrote for legendary music magazine *Creem*.

Pere Ubu's first two singles, '30 Seconds Over Tokyo' (b/w 'Heart of Darkness') and 'Final Solution' (b/w 'Cloud 149'), from 1975 and 1976 respectively, represent Laughner's only studio-recorded output. However, he left behind a vast collection of live, rehearsal and demo recordings, some of which are available on *The Day The Earth Met The Rocket From The Tombs* (2002). Other recordings, including solo acoustic work (Laughner was also involved in folk and roots music), are only available on hard-to-obtain bootlegs. A long-promised retrospective Laughner box set is still unreleased at the time of writing. Laughner died at the age of 24 of acute pancreatitis after years of heavy alcohol and drug use.

DATE OF BIRTH

22 August 1952

DATE OF DEATH

22 June 1977

GENRES

Experimental rock

ONLY THE
GOOD DIE YOUNG

RUDY LEWIS

SILKY-VOICED SOUL SINGER

Born in Philadelphia, Pennsylvania, Rudy Lewis (pictured on the far right) began his career in gospel music with The Clara Ward Singers, before auditioning for The Drifters in late 1960. He was hired on the spot, and occupied the position of lead singer from then until 1964, occasionally sharing those duties with Johnny Moore.

His silky voice graced The Drifters' hits such as 'Some Kind of Wonderful', 'Please Stay' and 'On Broadway'. Although he never quite achieved the same recognition as Ben E. King, his predecessor in the role, many hold him in as high regard as the founder of The Drifters, Clyde McPhatter, or King himself.

The group were booked in for a session to record 'Under the Boardwalk' on 21 May 1964. Lewis was found dead in his hotel room that morning, having died sometime the previous night. The cause of his death is unknown. Some claim it was a drug overdose, but others maintain that Lewis, a binge eater, choked to death in his sleep. Johnny Moore took over lead vocalist duties on the booked session, and 'Under the Boardwalk' became one of The Drifters' biggest hits.

DATE OF BIRTH

23 August 1936

DATE OF DEATH

20 May 1964

GENRES

R&B, doo-wop, soul

ONLY THE
GOOD DIE YOUNG

LITTLE WILLIE JOHN

R&B PIONEER

William Edward John, known as 'Little Willie' on account of his short stature, began his career in the family gospel group and was signed to King Records in 1955, producing a string of R&B hits over the next six years.

'Need Your Love So Bad' was a hit for Fleetwood Mac in 1968, but it was Little Willie who recorded the original in 1956, reaching No. 5 in the US R&B charts. 'Fever', memorably covered by Peggy Lee in 1958, was released by Little Willie two years earlier, and even though Lee's version was a much bigger hit, Little Willie's original still sold over a million copies and earned him a gold disc.

Known for his drinking and short temper, Little Willie was convicted of manslaughter in 1966. He was released while an appeal was considered, and recorded what was intended to be a comeback album (finally released in 2008 under the title *Nineteen Sixty Six*). His appeal failed and he died in Washington State Penitentiary, officially of a heart attack, although there are those who claim he may have been asphyxiated.

DATE OF BIRTH

15 November 1937

DATE OF DEATH

26 May 1968

GENRES

R&B, rock'n'roll

LISA 'LEFT EYE' LOPES

FOUNDER MEMBER OF TLC

Flamboyant and outspoken, rapper Lisa 'Left Eye' Lopes was best known for her work with the female vocal trio TLC, whose enticing blend of pop and hip-hop led them to superstardom in the 1990s.

Lopes was born in Philadelphia, Pennsylvania. The family moved around a lot due to her father's job in the United States Army. She finally settled in Atlanta, Georgia, in 1990, where she formed a trio with Tionne Watkins and Crystal Jones, originally called Second Nature. Successfully auditioning for R&B singer Perri 'Pebbles' Reid, who was to become their manager, the group was renamed TLC, an acronym formed from the three girls' first names. Crystal Jones was soon replaced by Rozonda Thomas (who was nicknamed 'Chilli' for the sake of the acronym). Signed to LaFace, they lost no time in beginning work on their first album.

SUPERSTARDOM

Oooooohhh ... On The TLC Tip (1992) proved to be a commercial success, providing the group with several hit singles – 'Ain't 2 Proud 2 Beg' (1991), 'Baby, Baby, Baby' (1992) and 'What About Your Friends' (1992) – and being certified quadruple platinum within a year. But it was their second album, *CrazySexyCool* (1994), that lifted them into the stratosphere, eventually selling over 11 million copies. This release showcased a more fluid and mature sound to their music, which clearly went down well with the record-buying public, spawning four hit singles – 'Creep' (1994), 'Red Light Special' (1995), 'Waterfalls' (1995) and 'Diggin' on You' (1995).

ONLY THE
GOOD DIE YOUNG

Lopes had had troubles with alcohol since the age of 15, but her drinking and her tumultuous private life had exploded into public view when she was arrested for burning down the house of her then-boyfriend, Andre Rison, shortly before the release of *CrazySexyCool*. She was sentenced to five years' probation and spent time in rehab.

LATER YEARS

Despite the huge success of *CrazySexyCool*, TLC filed for bankruptcy in 1995, and then problems between the group and producer Dallas Austin in 1997 brought preliminary work on the third album to a halt. Although these issues would eventually be resolved, it would be 1999 before *Fanmail* was released. During this hiatus, Lopes worked with a range of artists, most notably the R&B trio Blaque, who signed to her production company Left Eye Productions.

Tensions had been rising within TLC, however, with insults being publicly swapped between Lopes and Thomas. The band did not officially split, but Lopes spent much of her time after the *Fanmail* tour working on her solo album, *Supernova*, released in the UK in 2001, but not released in the US due to poor sales of the first single, 'The Block Party'. Undaunted, she signed with Suge Knight's Tha Row label and began work on a second solo album under the name N.I.N.A. Sessions had also begun on TLC's fourth album, *3D* (2002), when Lopes went to Honduras, where she was killed in a car crash on 25 April 2002.

DATE OF BIRTH

27 May 1971

DATE OF DEATH

25 April 2002

GENRES

R&B, hip-hop

ONLY THE
GOOD DIE YOUNG

FRANKIE LYMON

TEENAGE SINGING SENSATION

Despite the fame of Frankie Lymon & The Teenagers resting largely on one song, 'Why Do Fools Fall in Love' (1956), the group has had a lasting impact on popular music, forming the template for a large number of later vocal groups, most notably The Jackson Five. The story of a singer becoming famous at an early age for singing clean-cut songs whilst actually leading a far more dissolute life is sadly also all too common.

Lymon was born in Harlem, New York. The family were far from wealthy, and Lymon had to begin working part-time as a grocery boy at the age of 10 in order to help make ends meet. At the age of 13, he was invited to join a vocal group called The Premieres, featuring Jimmy Merchant, Sherman Garnes, Herman Santiago and Joe Negroni.

THE TEENAGERS

A neighbour had given the original quartet some love letters as inspiration for their own material, and they had been struggling to write a song called 'Why Do Birds Sing So Gay?'. Lymon helped them to rewrite the tune, and gave the song its far more inspired title, 'Why Do Fools Fall in Love'. Richard Barrett, who lived above the grocery shop where Lymon worked, sang with a group called The Valentines, who were under contract to Rama Records. Barrett arranged an audition with Rama owner George Goldner. Santiago, the group's original lead vocalist, was late for the audition, and so Lymon took his place.

The quintet, now named The Teenagers, were signed to Gee Records, and 'Why Do Fools Fall in Love' was released in January 1956. It was an instant success, topping the *Billboard* R&B singles chart for five weeks, and making No. 6

in the mainstream pop singles chart. With their second single, 'I Want you To Be My Girl' (1956), the group began to be billed as Frankie Lymon & The Teenagers, cementing his pre–eminent position in the group.

GOING SOLO

Altogether The Teenagers had five singles reach the *Billboard* R&B Top 10. Their album *Frankie Lymon & The Teenagers* was released in December 1956. But sales for their singles went into steady decline, and Lymon began to be pushed as a solo act. Indeed, the last single released as Frankie Lymon & The Teenagers, 'Goody Goody' (1957) was actually recorded by Lymon and a backing band. Another album, *Frankie Lymon At The London Palladium*, was released in 1957. But his solo career was not successful, going even further into decline after his voice broke and he lost the distinctive soprano that had graced the early hits.

Despite his clean–cut image, Lymon had been addicted to heroin since the age of 15, and as his success faded, his habit worsened. He entered a drug rehabilitation programme in 1961. In 1965, still only 22 years old, he enlisted in the army in lieu of a jail sentence for a heroin charge, but was dishonourably discharged. He travelled to New York in mid–February 1968 to discuss a possible return to recording, but was found dead of a heroin overdose in the house in Harlem where he had grown up.

DATE OF BIRTH

30 September 1942

DATE OF DEATH

27 February 1968

GENRES

Rock'n'roll, R&B

ONLY THE
GOOD DIE YOUNG

JIMMY McCULLOCH

PRECOCIOUS GUITAR TALENT

Scottish guitarist and songwriter Jimmy McCulloch is perhaps best known for playing with Wings from 1974 until 1977, but he had been at the centre of the British music scene for many years before then. His band One In A Million supported The Who in Scotland in 1967, and he had a No. 1 with band Thunderclap Newman ('Something in the Air') in 1969 at the tender age of 16.

Thunderclap Newman disbanded in 1971, and later that year McCulloch played with John Mayall & The Bluesbreakers. The Jimmy McCulloch Band was formed at the same time and toured in 1972. During this period, he did session work for the likes of Harry Nilsson and John Entwistle. Before joining Wings, he also played for Stone The Crows, replacing Les Harvey.

After leaving Wings in 1977, he played for the reformed Small Faces, touring with them and playing on their album '78 In The Shade (1978) and formed the band Wild Horses. His last recorded song, 'Heartbreaker', appeared on The Dukes' eponymous 1979 album. Jimmy McCulloch died from a heroin overdose at the age of 26.

DATE OF BIRTH

4 June 1953

DATE OF DEATH

27 September 1979

GENRES

Rock, hard rock

ROBBIE McINTOSH

SCOTTISH FUNK DRUMMER

Hailing from Dundee, drummer Robbie McIntosh played with white soul covers band The Senate and Brian Auger's Oblivion Express, appearing on *Oblivion Express* and *Better Land* (both 1971) and *Second Wind* (1972), before becoming a founder member of The Average White Band (AWB).

Formed in 1972, AWB's breakthrough was a support slot at Eric Clapton's comeback concert in 1973. Although their first album *Show Your Hand* (1973), released by MCA Records, sold poorly, Clapton's tour manager Bruce McCaskill agreed to promote them in the US and they were signed to Atlantic. Their follow-up album for Atlantic, *AWB* (also known as 'The White Album') topped the US *Billboard* Hot 100 in 1974.

At a party following a concert at the Troubadour in Los Angeles in September of that year, McIntosh and bandmate Alan Gorrie took what they believed to be cocaine. It was in fact heroin. The mistake cost McIntosh his life, and Gorrie only survived due to the intervention of fellow partygoer Cher. 'Pick Up The Pieces' from *AWB*, driven by McIntosh's razor-sharp drum patterns, reached the top of the *Billboard* charts the very next year.

DATE OF BIRTH

6 May 1950

DATE OF DEATH

23 September 1974

GENRES

Soul, funk, disco

ONLY THE
GOOD DIE YOUNG

RON 'PIGPEN' McKERNAN

FOUNDER MEMBER OF THE GRATEFUL DEAD

Ronald McKernan (pictured on the far right) was a pivotal figure in the early history of The Grateful Dead, bringing an earthy blues sensibility to the band's sound, grounding their increasingly extravagant excursions into psychedelia. His accomplished harmonica playing and authentic blues voice were vital contributions to the band, and are sorely missed by Deadheads to this day.

McKernan was born in San Bruno, California. Due to his father's work as an R&B DJ, he developed an early connection with the blues and black culture in general. He taught himself to play blues piano, but it was as a harmonica player and vocalist that he first began jamming with Jerry Garcia, playing with Mother McCree's Uptown Jug Champions and The Warlocks, the bands that finally morphed into The Grateful Dead, who played their first gig in December 1965 at one of Ken Kesey's Acid Tests.

LEAD SINGER

In the early days of The Grateful Dead, with other members of the band still shy about performing, McKernan was the focus of their live shows. His natural stage presence, however, masked a shyness of his own, and he was not able to take to the stage without loosening himself up by drinking. Concentrating more on the electric organ than the harmonica, he was responsible for the large number of blues tunes in the band's repertoire, including 'Turn On Your Love Light' (originally recorded by Bobby Bland in 1961), which regularly closed Grateful Dead shows, sometimes lasting 40 minutes or more.

ONLY THE
GOOD DIE YOUNG

Although the band became increasingly well known for their spectacular improvisatory live shows, McKernan participated on a series of studio albums, from 1967's *The Grateful Dead*, through *Anthem Of The Sun* (1968), *Aoxomoxoa* (1969) and *Workingman's Dead* (1970), to *American Beauty* (1970). The band also released several live double and triple albums during this period featuring McKernan: *Live/Dead* (1969), *Grateful Dead* (1971) and *Europe '72* (1972). McKernan had a brief relationship with Janis Joplin in the summer of 1966, whilst Big Brother & The Holding Company were living in California, the two singing together at a few shows around this time.

ILL HEALTH

Whilst others in the band experimented heavily with psychedelics, McKernan stuck firmly with booze. The increasing prominence of experimental psychedelia in The Grateful Dead's music, and the addition of keyboardist Tom Constanten to the line-up, led to McKernan being increasingly side-lined, often reduced to playing congas after leaving the band for a short while in 1968.

'Turn On Your Love Light' ensured he kept his place in the band during 1969, and when Constanten left the band in 1970, McKernan returned to the keyboard chair. The years of heavy drinking were catching up with him, however, and he was advised to stop touring after being hospitalized in August 1971. He rejoined the band in December that year, alongside new pianist Keith Godchaux, but he proved too ill to continue for long and he made his final concert appearance on 17 June 1972. He was found dead of a gastrointestinal haemorrhage at his home in California on 8 March 1973.

DATE OF BIRTH

8 September 1945

DATE OF DEATH

8 March 1973

GENRES

Psychedelic rock, blues rock, jam rock

ONLY THE
GOOD DIE YOUNG

JACOB MILLER

REGGAE VOCALIST

Jacob Miller was born in Mandeville, Jamaica, and moved to Kingston at the age of eight, where he lived with his grandparents. He began to spend time at Clement Dodd's Studio One, where he recorded three songs, one of which, 1968's 'Love is a Message', came to the attention of musician and record producer Augustus Pablo, who recorded five more Miller songs between 1972 and 1974.

Inner Circle recruited Miller to lead vocals for their 1974 album, *Rock The Boat*, and he sang on seven subsequent albums released by the band. Inner Circle were known for experimenting with a range of styles, including soul, funk and disco, as well as reggae. In the solo work that he continued to produce, however, Miller concentrated on his favoured rockers style, producing his first solo album, *Tenement Yard*, in 1976.

Miller's final album, *Mixed Up Moods* (1979), had just been pressed and Inner Circle were preparing for an American tour with Bob Marley & The Wailers when Miller was killed in a car accident on Hope Road in Kingston at the age of 27.

DATE OF BIRTH

4 May 1952

DATE OF DEATH

23 March 1980

GENRES

Reggae

ONLY THE
GOOD DIE YOUNG

KEITH MOON

THE WILD MAN OF ROCK

Whilst Keith Moon was notorious for his hard-drinking, wild-partying life of rock'n'roll excess, his true legacy is as one of the finest rock drummers there has ever been. His flamboyant signature style, coupled with his technique of playing with the guitar rather than the bass, liberated his playing from a mere time-keeping role, and pushed the drums to the forefront of The Who's sound.

Keith John Moon was born in Wembley, London. Moon joined the local Sea Cadet band on bugle, but soon switched to the drums after his father bought him his first kit at the age of 14. He played drums in local outfits The Escorts and The Beachcombers, before joining The Who at the age of 17.

THE WHO

From July to October 1964, The Who changed their name to The High Numbers, releasing the single 'Zoot Suit/I'm the Face'. But the band only found their musical form after changing their name back to The Who and releasing 'I Can't Explain' in 1965. Prior to this release, Pete Townshend had accidentally broken his guitar at a gig. In response to laughs from the audience, he smashed the instrument up, and this destruction of instruments, enthusiastically adopted by Moon, became an attraction of the band's early gigs.

The Who's debut album, *My Generation* (1965), spawned the singles 'My Generation' (1965) and 'The Kids Are Alright' (1966), with further hits from Townshend's pen following over the next few years. Subsequent albums

A Quick One (1966) and *The Who Sell Out* (1967) saw the band move in a more ambitious direction, with their albums becoming more thematically coherent, although still containing hit singles. This tendency culminated in *Tommy* (1969), the first rock opera.

SELF-DESTRUCTION

During an appearance on American TV show *The Smother Brothers Comedy Hour*, Moon managed to destroy his drum kit with explosives. Similar behaviour (with Moon showing an odd penchant for blowing up the toilets in hotel rooms) led to a reputation for extreme behaviour and gives the impression of a man who continually struggled to keep his manic energy in check. It was precisely this energy of course that propelled him to such extraordinary feats behind the drum kit.

Moon played on all releases by The Who up until his death, also making a small number of appearances on other musicians' records, recording a solo album, *Two Sides of the Moon* (1975) (with Moon however only playing drums on three tracks), and appearing in a number of films, including Frank Zappa's *200 Motels* (1971) and Ken Russell's film version of *Tommy* (1975). But his involvement in the accidental death of a friend in 1970 affected him deeply, and his lifestyle began to have serious effects on his health. Shortly after the release of *Who Are You* (1978), Moon died in the London flat of Harry Nilsson, ironically from an overdose of tablets prescribed to him to alleviate the symptoms of alcohol withdrawal.

DATE OF BIRTH

23 August 1946

DATE OF DEATH

7 September 1978

GENRES

Hard rock, art rock, power pop

ONLY THE
GOOD DIE YOUNG

JIM MORRISON

THE LIZARD KING

One of the iconic rock stars of the 1960s, Jim Morrison's combination of sexual energy and poetic leanings have led to him and his band The Doors exerting a remarkable influence even to this day. Morrison, born in Melbourne, Florida, suffered a peripatetic childhood due to his father's job in the US Navy. He read widely in his youth, with the influence of the 19th-century philosopher Friedrich Nietzsche and the symbolist poet Arthur Rimbaud especially apparent in his later work. He moved to Los Angeles in early 1964, completing a degree from the University of California, Los Angeles (UCLA) film school in 1965 and making several short films while studying there.

THE DOORS

After graduating from UCLA, Morrison formed The Doors with Ray Manzarek, John Densmore and Robby Krieger, taking the band's name from Aldous Huxley's book *The Doors Of Perception*. By June 1966, The Doors were opening for Van Morrison and his band Them at the Whisky a Go Go, and were signed to Elektra Records in August that year. Their debut album, *The Doors*, was recorded at the end of August 1966 and released in January 1967. The second single from that album, 'Light My Fire' (1967), was a hit and the band capitalized on its success with a string of bestselling albums – *Strange Days* (1967), *Waiting For The Sun* (1968), *The Soft Parade* (1969), *Morrison Hotel* (1970), the patchy double album *Absolutely Live* (1970) and *L.A. Woman* (1971).

An early appearance on the *Ed Sullivan Show* in late 1967, where Morrison refused (or forgot) to change the lyric 'girl we couldn't get much higher' in 'Light My Fire', was indicative of the controversy that surrounded Morrison's performances.

ONLY THE
GOOD DIE YOUNG

Morrison, the self-styled 'Lizard King', was always the undisputed focus of The Doors' live performances, and the pressures of the band's success, combined with his heavy drinking and a genuine interest in the artistic potential of provocation, led to his performances becoming increasingly erratic. Infamously, he was arrested in 1969 for indecent exposure at a concert in Miami.

AMERICAN POET

Morrison was not the first or the last rock lyricist to think of himself (and be thought of by others) as a poet, but his claim to such status was not entirely unfounded. He self-published two collections of his poetry in 1969, *The Lords/Notes On Vision* and *The New Creatures*, and two volumes of poems were published posthumously (*Wilderness* in 1988 and *The American Night* in 1990). There were also two recording sessions in 1969 and 1970 devoted to his poetry.

Taking, as he always had, Nietzsche's thoughts on Dionysus rather too much to heart, Morrison walked a tightrope between poetically inspired provocation and drunken boorishness, increasingly tipping from the former to the latter as his career progressed. Dissatisfied with the pressures of fame, Morrison and his long-term partner Pamela Courson flew to Paris in March 1971. He was found dead in his bathtub on 3 July, most likely killed by taking heroin after drinking heavily, although no autopsy was ever carried out.

DATE OF BIRTH

8 December 1943

DATE OF DEATH

3 July 1971

GENRES

Psychedelic rock, blues rock

ONLY THE
GOOD DIE YOUNG

BiLLY MURCiA

NEW YORK DOLLS' ORIGINAL DRUMMER

It is not known exactly when Billy Murcia (pictured second from the left) was born in Bogota, Colombia, but since most sources put his age at his death at 21, it is most likely to have been sometime in 1951. He grew up in Jackson Heights, New York, and while attending Quintano's School for Young Professionals, formed several short-lived bands with Sylvain Sylvain and Johnny Thunders between 1967 and 1970.

Murcia replaced the drummer of Thunders' new band, Actress, in 1971 and when David Johansen joined the band as lead singer, The New York Dolls were born. The band's debut performance was on Christmas Eve 1971, and they were soon playing their legendary series of weekly shows at New York's Mercer Arts Center.

Just as a bidding war was beginning amongst record company executives, Murcia passed out from an accidental overdose at a party in London. Attempts to revive him by putting him in a bathtub and force-feeding him coffee led to his asphyxiation and death. His drumming can be heard on the posthumously released *Lipstick Killers* (1981, re-released 2006).

DATE OF BIRTH

1951

DATE OF DEATH

6 November 1972

GENRES

Rock'n'roll, glam punk, glam rock, proto-punk

ONLY THE
GOOD DIE YOUNG

FATS NAVARRO

BEBOP PiONEER

Born in Key West, Florida, Fats Navarro graduated from high school and then hit the road with various touring big bands, including most notably Billy Eckstine's, where he replaced Dizzy Gillespie (at Gillespie's own suggestion).

In the time between Navarro's arrival in New York City in August 1946 and his death in 1950, he recorded around 150 sides in the small group format. Whether appearing as a featured sideman to players such as Coleman Hawkins, Bud Powell and Tadd Dameron, on sessions with lesser-known artists, or under his own name, Navarro always played beautifully, combining lyricism with breathtaking technical fluency.

By 1949, his heavy drug use and developing TB was slowing him down, and he only had two studio recording dates that year. Despite his increasing ill health, his final recordings from early 1950 show him more than holding his own against Charlie Parker and Bud Powell, but he was hospitalized on the 1 July 1950 and was dead less than a week later.

DATE OF BiRTH

24 September 1923

DATE OF DEATH

7 July 1950

GENRES

Bebop

ONLY THE
GOOD DiE YOUNG

THE NOTORIOUS B.I.G.

EAST COAST HIP-HOP STAR

Born Christopher George Latore Wallace, The Notorious B.I.G., also known as Biggie Smalls, did not have long in the limelight, but still managed to exert an enormous influence on hip-hop. He brought east coast rap back to prominence and perfected a peculiar mixture of exaggerated sexual and macho braggadocio with a disarming emotional honesty that painted a vivid picture of the life he knew growing up.

Born in Brooklyn, New York, Wallace's school career started well, but by the age of 12 he had begun dealing drugs, and he dropped out of school aged 17, finally spending nine months in jail in 1991 for dealing crack cocaine. But he had also been rapping, performing with The Old Gold Brothers and The Techniques, and after his release from jail made a demo tape that came to the attention of a certain Sean Combs (soon to find fame as Puff Daddy), then working for Uptown Records, who signed him to the label in early 1992.

DEBUT ALBUM

Combs left Uptown shortly after and started his own label, Bad Boy Records. Wallace followed him, soon making appearances on remixes of other artists' singles, most notably Mary J. Blige and Neneh Cherry. Although a solo track, 'Party and Bullshit', appeared on the soundtrack to the 1993 film *Who's The Man?*, it was not until August 1994 that he had his first solo chart success with the double A-side 'Juicy/Unbelievable'.

Wallace's debut album, *Ready To Die* (1994), followed in September, receiving strong reviews. Drawing on Wallace's earlier drug-dealing life for much of its lyrical content, it focused not only on the more clichéd gangsta tropes of guns

and women, but also, more interestingly, on the state of the protagonist's soul. The album was eventually certified quadruple platinum and remains a high point in the development of east coast rap.

LATER WORK

When Tupac Shakur was shot in New York in November 1994, he accused Wallace and Combs of involvement. Both Wallace and Combs strenuously denied the claim. Nevertheless, rivalry between Bad Boy Records and Suge Knight's Death Row, combined with the old tradition of insulting one's competitors in song, escalated the tensions between the east and west coast hip-hop camps, with Shakur and Wallace the totemic figures. Wallace spent 1995 concentrating on boosting the careers of childhood friends Junior M.A.F.I.A., guesting on two of their singles ('Player's Anthem' and 'Get Money') as well as working with Michael Jackson on the *HIStory* album and R. Kelly on the single '(You To Be) Happy'. 1996 saw Wallace involved in Lil' Kim's debut album, *Hard Core* (1996).

Wallace had begun work on his second album, *Life After Death* (1997), towards the end of 1995, but the process of recording was delayed by Wallace's involvement in other projects and also by a car accident that saw him confined to a wheelchair for a short period of time. By the time the album was released, Wallace was dead, shot in Los Angeles in a drive-by shooting bearing a chilling similarity to the murder of Tupac Shakur just six months earlier. The murder remains unsolved.

DATE OF BIRTH

21 May 1972

DATE OF DEATH

9 March 1997

GENRES

Hip-hop

ONLY THE
GOOD DIE YOUNG

BERRY OAKLEY

BASS PLAYER FOR THE ALLMAN BROTHERS

Raymond Berry Oakley III started off as a lead guitarist and only became a bass player after offering to stand in as bassist (despite not even owning a bass at the time) for Tommy Roe's backing band, The Roemans, when their regular bassist was drafted into the army. After Oakley moved to Florida, he joined Dicky Betts' band, The Second Coming. Shortly after, then–session guitarist Duane Allman asked Oakley and Betts to join his new band.

The resulting group, The Allman Brothers Band, soon landed a recording contract with Polydor and began touring incessantly. Their first two albums, *The Allman Brothers Band* (1969) and *Idlewild South* (1970), brought critical acclaim, but breakthrough success was not achieved until the 1971 live album *At Filimore East*. The band's blues rock sound and improvisatory ethos was underpinned by Oakley's sturdy bass lines. Just over a year after Duane Allman's death in a motorcycle accident, Oakley died in eerily similar circumstances, just three blocks from where his bandmate had met his end.

DATE OF BIRTH

4 April 1948

DATE OF DEATH

11 November 1972

GENRES

Southern rock

PHIL OCHS

POLITICAL FOLK SINGER

The politically charged atmosphere of 1960s America produced many folk singers with a social conscience, but few demonstrated the same conviction as Phil Ochs. Whilst Dylan quickly moved on from protest songs to the poetic maelstrom of his mid–Sixties work, Ochs struck to his guns. Whilst he did write non–political songs, he always remained involved in the causes he championed, combining artistry and commitment to a degree unmatched by any other songwriter of the time.

Born in El Paso, Texas, as a teenager Ochs played the clarinet, but the rock'n'roll of Elvis Presley and Buddy Holly soon caught his attention. Surprisingly, in view of his later political disposition, Ochs spent two years in the late 1950s at the Staunton Military Academy in Virginia. It was whilst studying journalism at Ohio State University that he met Jim Glover, who introduced Ochs to the music of Woody Guthrie and other folk singers and taught Ochs to play the guitar.

NEW YORK CITY

In 1961, Ochs began playing professionally at folk clubs in Cleveland, Ohio. The following year he dropped out of his college course and went to New York City to become a folk singer. Describing himself as a 'singing journalist', he performed at the Newport Folk Festival in 1963 and again in 1964. He continued writing, contributing articles as well as songs to *Broadside* magazine and becoming a contributing editor.

Ochs's reputation as a songwriter grew. Bob Dylan wrote in his 'A Letter From Bob Dylan' (*Broadside* #38, January 1964), 'As for Phil, I just can't keep up with him/an' he's getting' better an' better an' better'. Ochs' trio of albums

ONLY THE
GOOD DIE YOUNG

for Elektra – *All the News That's Fit To Sing* (1964), *I Ain't Marching Anymore* (1965) and *In Concert* (1966) (the last actually containing very little material recorded live) – contained many of his classic 'topical' songs (with 'Here's to the State of Mississippi' from *I Ain't Marching Anymore* perhaps the best example of his witty and caustic approach).

LATER WORK

1967 saw him sign to A&M Records and move to California, recording and releasing *Pleasures Of The Harbor*, which introduced far more ornate instrumentation and more introspective subject matter. The single 'Outside Of A Small Circle Of Friends' was hampered by many radio stations refusing to play it (mainly due to its reference to marijuana).

Further albums followed – *Tape From California* (1968), *Rehearsals For Retirement* (1969) and *Greatest Hits* (1970) (which contained only new material) – all of which continued to develop his new style, exemplified by his 1970 decision to be 'part Elvis Presley and part Che Guevara'. His political activity continued unabated, for example organizing a 1973 benefit to raise funds for the people of Chile in the aftermath of General Pinochet's coup, at which he managed to persuade his old sparring partner Bob Dylan to appear.

Throughout the early 1970s, however, Ochs' muse began to desert him, his drinking became more and more of a problem and his behaviour became increasingly erratic. He moved in with his sister in Far Rockaway, New York, in January 1976, where he was diagnosed with manic depression (as bipolar disorder was then known). He hanged himself at his sister's house in April the same year.

DATE OF BIRTH

19 December 1940

DATE OF DEATH

9 April 1976

GENRES

Folk, folk rock

ONLY THE
GOOD DIE YOUNG

OL' DiRTY BASTARD

TROUBLED RAPPER WiTH THE WU-TANG CLAN

Brooklyn-born Ol' Dirty Bastard (real name Russell Jones) formed the group Force Of The Imperial Master with his cousins Robert Diggs and Gary Grice, which became All In Together Now, and finally, with the addition of further members, Wu-Tang Clan, releasing *Enter The Wu-Tang (36 Chambers)* in 1993.

Their debut was critically acclaimed and is now regarded as one of the greatest hip-hop albums of all time, but it was 1997's *Wu-Tang Forever* that proved to be their commercial breakthrough. Like the other members of the Wu-Tang Clan, Jones released several solo albums, including *Return To The 36 Chambers (Dirty Version)* in 1995 and *Nigga Please* in 1999. *A Son Unique*, although recorded in 2003 and 2004, has not yet been released.

Known for his off-beat rhymes and vocal inflections, and increasingly for his erratic behaviour, legal troubles led to Jones only appearing once on the Wu-Tang Clan's next group album, *The W* (2000), and not at all on 2001's *Iron Flag*. Jones collapsed from a drug overdose at the group's recording studios on 13 November 2004 and was pronounced dead shortly after.

DATE OF BiRTH

15 Nov 1968

DATE OF DEATH

13 Nov 2004

GENRES

Hip-hop

CHARLIE PARKER

BEBOP INNOVATOR

Saxophonist Charlie 'Bird' Parker was pivotal in the development of bebop, the harmonically sophisticated development of jazz that emerged in the 1940s. Given the quantity of his output on disc, his recording career was surprisingly short, but he was largely responsible for overthrowing the commercialism of the swing era and establishing jazz as a music worthy of serious appreciation.

Born in Kansas City, Kansas, and moving at an early age to Kansas City, Missouri, Parker began playing saxophone at the age of 11. In 1939 Parker moved to New York City, then the centre of the jazz world, making his professional recording debut with Jay McShann's band in 1940.

DEVELOPMENT OF BEBOP

Parker claimed in the 1950s that it was while playing in a jam session in New York in 1939 that his ideas about harmonic structure crystallized, finally allowing him to play the music that he heard in his head. In the early years, the new style of playing – of which Dizzy Gillespie was another early exponent and which soon became known as 'bebop' – was largely worked out in after-hours jam sessions. By the time it was ready to be filtered into the recording studios of New York City, a Musicians Union recording ban was in place (the ban ran from 1942 until 1944), and so there is little evidence of the early development of this innovative jazz style.

Parker led his own group for the first time in 1945 and also played extensively with Dizzy Gillespie. In December of that year Parker and Gillespie travelled to Los Angeles, playing a six-week nightclub engagement, although Parker remained

in Los Angeles recording and performing until the end of June 1946, when a breakdown, alongside his alcohol and heroin use, led to him being committed to Camarillo State Hospital for six months.

JAZZ STAR

On his return to New York in April 1947, Parker formed a quintet with Miles Davis, Duke Jordan, Tommy Potter and Max Roach that produced what many consider to be Parker's best work. But he was extremely busy over the next four years, recording with a wide variety of musicians, including Afro–Cuban bands, and even laying down two albums with strings, both confusingly called *Charlie Parker With Strings* (1949 and 1950). Although some jazz fans accused Parker of selling out, Parker himself considered the version of 'Just Friends' from the 1949 session his best recording.

Parker's New York cabaret licence was revoked from 1951 to 1953, making it difficult for him to find work, and he twice attempted suicide in 1954. Appearing on stage for the last time at Birdland, the New York jazz club named in his honour, on 5 March 1955, he died a week later in the Manhattan apartment of his friend and patron, Baroness Pannonica de Koenigswarter. The doctor who performed his autopsy estimated the body to be of a man between 50 and 60 years of age; he was 34. He left behind him a body of work that represents a defining moment in the history of jazz, and continues to provide inspiration to jazz musicians today.

DATE OF BiRTH

29 August 1920

DATE OF DEATH

12 March 1955

GENRES

Jazz, bebop

GRAM PARSONS
COSMIC AMERICAN MUSICIAN

Musical innovators who bring together previously disparate music genres are seldom rewarded by commercial success, and such was the fate of Gram Parsons, whose blending of country and rock failed to find a wide audience amongst fans of either genre during his lifetime. His influence has continued to grow in the years since his death, however, and his music, called 'Cosmic American Music' by Parsons himself, is now recognized as an important stage in the development of country rock and the foundation of alt-country.

Born Ingram Cecil Connor III into a wealthy Florida family, Parsons' childhood was nevertheless far from idyllic. His father committed suicide when he was just 12 years old, and his mother died from cirrhosis in 1965 on the very day he graduated from high school. Seeing Elvis Presley in concert led to a strong interest in music, and he played in a wide variety of covers and folk bands in his youth.

INTERNATIONAL SUBMARINE BAND AND THE BYRDS

While attending Harvard to study theology in 1966 (he only lasted one semester), Parsons (he took his stepfather's name in the late 1950s) formed the International Submarine Band. The band moved to Los Angeles in 1967 and recorded *Safe at Home*, released on LHI Records in mid-1968. By this time the band had broken up, with Parsons already playing with The Byrds.

Initially auditioning as a pianist, Parsons soon became The Byrds' rhythm guitarist and co-vocalist. He appeared on the 1968 Byrds album *Sweetheart Of The Rodeo*, although due to contractual disputes with LHI Records, three of

ONLY THE
GOOD DIE YOUNG

his lead vocals on the record were replaced by Roger McGuinn. Parsons influenced the entire album, however, turning it into a country music project and persuading the band to record it in Nashville, Tennessee.

BURRITO BROTHERS AND SOLO WORK

After leaving The Byrds, apparently due to concern at their forthcoming tour of South Africa, Parsons formed The Flying Burrito Brothers. Their debut *The Gilded Palace of Sin* (1969) was well received by the critics, but the band's combination of country, rock, blues and soul mystified many audiences. Time spent partying with The Rolling Stones hardly contributed to Parsons' songwriting, but it did lead to an opening set at the Altamont Music Festival in 1969. It was at this point that Parsons met Phil Kaufman, who was to become Parsons' road manager and friend. The band's second album, *Burrito Deluxe*, was released in 1970, after which Parsons left the band.

Kicking heroin (at least for a time) allowed Parsons to return to form with his first solo album, *GP* (1973), touring with Emmylou Harris as Gram Parsons & The Fallen Angels. *Grievous Angel* was Parsons' final album, released posthumously in 1974. Parsons died on 19 September 1973 in a motel in Joshua Tree National Park from an overdose of drugs and alcohol. Despite an attempt by his stepfather to ship his body to Louisiana, Kaufman and friend Michael Martin managed to steal his body and cremate it in the Joshua Tree National Park, honouring an agreement made between Parsons and Kaufman at the funeral of Clarence White earlier in the year.

DATE OF BIRTH

5 November 1946

DATE OF DEATH

19 September 1973

GENRES

Rock, bluegrass, country rock

ONLY THE
GOOD DIE YOUNG

JACO PASTORIUS
THE GREATEST BASS PLAYER IN THE WORLD

Jaco Pastorius, unencumbered by false modesty, used to refer to himself as 'the greatest bass player in the word', but in his case the boast was probably accurate. He was noteworthy for developing the potential of the electric bass as an instrument in its own right, and for demonstrating that a bass player could have a role far beyond the rhythm section.

John Francis Pastorius III was born in Norristown, Pennsylvania, although he moved with his family to Florida shortly after his birth. His nickname was inspired by his love of sports, 'Jaco' being a misspelling of 'Jocko'. Pastorius began as a drummer, only switching to the bass after sustaining a sporting injury. He started on a cheap electric bass, and after a spell on an upright, finally acquired his trademark 1960 Fender Jazz electric bass.

DEBUT SOLO RELEASE

Pastorius picked up work with Wayne Cochran & The C.C. Riders, and turned up on a few records by various Florida jazz and R&B players, but in 1974 he began playing with Pat Metheny, the pair recording the album *Bright Size Life* (1976) with drummer Bob Moses, a record which marks the beginning of Pastorius' distinctive contribution to the jazz bass.

It was his standout debut solo album, *Jaco Pastorius*, released in 1976, that truly put him on the map. Featuring a host of jazz luminaries including Herbie Hancock, Wayne Shorter and Michael Brecker, and containing the standout solo bass track 'Portrait of Tracy', it was a breathtaking debut that in one fell swoop established the electric bass as a serious soloing instrument and brought Pastorius to wider notice.

Pastorius joined Weather Report after meeting keyboard player Josef Zawinul, appearing on two tracks on their 1976 album *Black Market*. This was the beginning of an intensely creative period for Pastorius and the band. *Heavy Weather* (1977) combined strong sales with critical acclaim. *Mr Gone* (1978) was less successful with the critics, but still went gold and features Pastorius on drums on two of the tracks. The 1979 live double album *8:30* captures the classic slim–line Weather Report line–up of Wayne Shorter, Peter Erskine, Zawinul and Pastorius at the height of their powers, and *Night Passage* (1980) captures the quartet live with the addition of percussionist Robert Thomas Jr. *Weather Report* (1982) was Pastorius' last album with the band. By the time of its release, Pastorius had released his second solo album, *Word Of Mouth* (1981).

BESIDES WEATHER REPORT

During this period, Pastorius had also appeared on a number of releases by other artists, most notably collaborating with Joni Mitchell on four albums – *Hejira* (1976), *Don Juan's Reckless Daughter* (1977), *Mingus* (1979) and the live album *Shadows And Light* (1980).

Work was done on a recording project, *Holiday For Pans*, in late 1982, with Pastorius composing and producing rather than playing bass. Widely bootlegged, it has never been released. Pastorius' behaviour was by this stage becoming increasingly erratic, and he was diagnosed with manic depression. He spent some time in hospital and even endured various periods living on the streets, before falling into a coma in September 1987 after a violent confrontation with a club bouncer.

DATE OF BIRTH

1 December 1951

DATE OF DEATH

21 September 1987

GENRES

Jazz, jazz fusion

ONLY THE
GOOD DIE YOUNG

KRISTEN PFAFF

GRUNGE BASSIST

Kristen Pfaff (pictured second from the right) was born in Buffalo, New York, and studied classical piano from the age of five to 14. It was while studying at the University of Minnesota in Minneapolis that she began playing the bass guitar and joined Janitor Joe, a three-piece band that released several singles and an album, *Big Metal Birds* (1993), while Pfaff was with them.

While touring in California, Pfaff was scouted for Hole, and although she initially declined to join, she later relented, moving to Seattle, Washington in 1993, and appearing on the band's second album, *Live Through This*. Hole guitarist Eric Erlanson has claimed that it was with Pfaff's recruitment that Hole 'became a real band'.

Pfaff developed a problem with heroin, entering rehab in late 1993. In spring 1994, she took time off from Hole to tour again with Janitor Joe, returning apparently drug free. After Kurt Cobain's death in April 1994, Pfaff decided to leave Hole and Seattle and return to Minneapolis to play permanently with Janitor Joe. She never made it. She was found dead in the bath of her apartment, her death attributed to acute opiate intoxication.

DATE OF BIRTH

26 May 1976

DATE OF DEATH

16 June 1994

GENRES

Alternative rock, punk rock

RIVER PHOENIX

ACTOR AND MUSICIAN

Better known as an actor, River Phoenix's true passion was music. In 1976 when his family were missionaries in Venezuela, Phoenix and his sister Rain would sing and play guitar on street corners in order to provide food for the family. By 1979, the family were back in the US, and Phoenix and Rain were playing talent shows around the Florida area.

It was the acting career that took off, of course, although Phoenix recorded a song, 'Heart to Get', for the end credits of *A Night In The Life Of Jimmy Reardon* (1986) (the song was cut for the film's initial release). During filming, however, Phoenix met Chris Blackwell of Island Records who gave him a development deal. Phoenix formed the band Aleka's Attic, which also included his sister Rain.

The band released 'Across the Way' (1989), and the track 'Too Many Colors' was used on the soundtrack of *My Own Private Idaho* (1991), which also starred Phoenix. Phoenix died of drug-induced heart failure outside a Los Angeles nightclub in 1993.

DATE OF BIRTH

23 August 1970

DATE OF DEATH

31 October 1993

GENRES

Alternative folk, alternative rock

ONLY THE
GOOD DIE YOUNG

TOSE PROESKI

BALKAN SUPERSTAR

Proeski was born in Prilep, in what is today Macedonia. His first public performance was at the age of 12, and from 1996 he began performing at festivals across Macedonia. 1999 saw the release of his debut album, *Nekade vo Nokta (Somewhere In The Night)*, and the follow-up, *Sinot Bozji (The Son Of God)*, was released in 2000. After touring Australia with other Macedonian singers in 2001, Proeski recorded his third album, *Ako Me Poglednes Vo Oci (If You Look Into My Eyes)*, in late 2002.

He took singing classes in New York with William Riley, who was also coach to Luciano Pavarotti, and when he was selected to represent Macedonia at the Eurovision Song Contest in 2004, he took to singing opera at his press conferences.

Named a UNICEF Goodwill Ambassador in 2004, Proeski recorded 'This World', which became the UNICEF anthem. 2006's *Bozilak (Rainbow)* was a collection of traditional Macedonian folk songs. Proeski wrote several of his hits, and also wrote Macedonia's entry in the 2005 Eurovision Song Contest. He died in a car accident.

DATE OF BIRTH

25 January 1981

DATE OF DEATH

16 October 2007

GENRES

World, pop, rock, classical

ONLY THE
GOOD DIE YOUNG

JAY REATARD

GARAGE PUNK SINGER AND GUITARIST

Jay Reatard (real name Jimmy Lee Lindsey Jr) was a prolific singer and songwriter from Memphis, Tennessee. He played and recorded with a bewildering array of bands, many of them short-lived, but is best known for his work with The Reatards and The Lost Sounds, and as a solo artist.

Lindsey's first release, *Get Real Stupid* (1998), under The Reatards name but featuring only Lindsey, was soon followed by the albums *Teenage Hate* (1998) and *Grown Up Fucked Up* (1999) with The Reatards now a trio. The new century saw a side project, The Lost Sounds, become the main outlet for Lindsey's music, although he continued to contribute to and record with The Reatards and other projects such as The Final Solutions, Nervous Patterns and Bad Times.

By 2006, with both The Reatards and The Lost Sounds broken up, Lindsey was concentrating on solo work, releasing *Blood Visions* in 2006 and *Matador Singles '08* in 2008. His final album, *Watch Me Fall* (2009), was seeing his work become more melodic. Lindsey died in his sleep in early 2010, with cocaine and alcohol contributing factors.

DATE OF BIRTH

1 May 1980

DATE OF DEATH

13 January 2010

GENRES

Punk rock, indie rock

OTIS REDDING

THE KING OF SOUL

Otis Redding was one of the most successful songwriters and soul singers of the late 1960s, bringing to his music a gravel-voiced earthiness more reminiscent of early blues shouters and rock'n'roll pioneers such as Little Richard than the increasingly smooth style favoured by soul singers of the time. He had a string of hits, with his best-known song, '(Sittin' On) The Dock Of The Bay' (1968), only released after his death.

Otis Ray Redding Jr born in Dawson, Georgia, left school at 15 to sing with Little Richard's backing band The Upsetters, Little Richard remaining an inspiration to Redding for the rest of his career. Redding also entered local talent shows from which he was eventually banned because he would win with such regularity.

A VOICE OF HIS OWN

His first recordings were 'She's Alright/Tuff Enough' (1960) as Otis & The Shooters, and 'Shout Bamalama/Fat Girl' (1960) with The Pinetoppers, the band with which he toured as a driver and musician. But it was with a recording of his own composition, 'These Arms of Mine' (1962), that he began to make his mark. This record, released on Stax subsidiary Volt Records, was successful enough for him to record in Memphis with the Stax house band Booker T & The MGs, and he released his debut album *Pain In My Heart* in 1964.

A concert at the Apollo Theatre in New York at the end of 1963 proved to be a turning point in his career, and the hits began in earnest in 1965 and 1966, which saw 'Mr Pitiful', 'I've Been Loving You Too Long', 'I Can't Turn You Loose', 'Satisfaction' and 'Respect' (later memorably covered by Aretha Franklin) all selling well.

ONLY THE
GOOD DIE YOUNG

Redding's continuing success helped develop the reputation of Stax, and high-profile fans of the label's distinctive sound such as The Beatles encouraged Redding to reach out to white audiences. Gigs at venues such as the Whisky a Go Go in Los Angeles helped him achieve this. 'Try A Little Tenderness' – after 'Dock Of The Bay' perhaps Redding's best-known recording (although it is not written by Redding and dates from 1932) – features on the album *Complete And Unbelievable: The Otis Redding Dictionary Of Soul* (1966).

A CHANGE OF APPROACH

Although *Complete And Unbelievable* was the last solo album Redding released before his death, the album *King & Queen*, where Redding duets with Carla Thomas, was released in 1967. He joined long-term collaborator (and MGs guitarist) Steve Cropper in the Stax studio in November 1967 to work on a song that Redding had started writing while staying in California in August. Some were concerned that '(Sittin' On) The Dock Of The Bay' did not fit in with the rest of Redding's output, and although it did mark a change of direction, Redding said that he fully intended it to be a little different from his other material. No one ever got to find out whether the song would mark a permanent shift in Redding's approach, since he was killed in a plane crash on 10 December on his way to a gig.

DATE OF BIRTH

9 September 1941

DATE OF DEATH

10 December 1967

GENRES

Soul

KEITH RELF

LEAD SINGER WITH THE YARDBIRDS

Relf is best known as a member of the enormously influential Yardbirds. His powerful lead vocals and harmonica playing, combined with his songwriting ability, meant that Relf was a vital contributor to the band that formed the template for guitar-driven experimental blues rock. As well as a string of singles, the band released one studio album (*Yardbirds* from 1966), one live album (*Five Live Yardbirds*, 1964) and two EPs (*Five Yardbirds*, 1965 and *Over Under Sideways Down*, 1967) in the UK.

After The Yardbirds split in 1968, Relf worked with fellow Yardbird Jim McCarty in acoustic duo Together, and then the experimental classical/folk/rock quintet Renaissance, which also featured Relf's sister Jane. They released their eponymous debut in 1969. After the original line-up finally dissolved in late 1970, the follow-up, *Illusion*, was not released in the UK until 1976.

During the rest of the early 1970s, Relf was involved in various projects, producing and playing bass for Medicine Head, providing backing vocals for Steamhammer, and playing with heavy rock band Armageddon. Relf died at home from electrocution whilst playing his electric guitar.

DATE OF BIRTH

22 March 1943

DATE OF DEATH

14 May 1976

GENRES

Blues rock, folk rock, psychedelic rock

ONLY THE
GOOD DIE YOUNG

THE REV

DRUMMER WITH AVENGED SEVENFOLD

James Owen Sullivan (more commonly known by the stage name The Reverend Tholomew Plague, or The Rev) was the drummer for third-wave ska band Suburban Legends, appearing on their home-produced album *Origin Edition* (1999), before leaving to become a founder member of metalcore/hard-rock band Avenged Sevenfold.

Following two demos in 1999 and 2000, Avenged Sevenfold released their debut, *Sounding The Seventh Trumpet*, in 2001. The band's style evolved from these metal-core beginnings to the more classic metal sound of *City Of Evil* (2005) and subsequent releases. Sullivan's distinctive style, which he called 'double-ride', was indicative of his eclectic influences, including Frank Zappa and drummers such as Vinnie Paul and Lars Ulrich. Sullivan was also a vocalist, songwriter and piano player for the band. He took on lead vocal and piano playing duties in side-project Pinkly Smooth with Avenged Sevenfold guitarist Synyster Gates; they released one album, *Unfortunate Snort* (2002) before disbanding. His death at the age of 28 was initially reported as due to natural causes, but later transpired to have been due to acute multiple-drug intoxication.

DATE OF BIRTH

9 February 1981

DATE OF DEATH

28 December 2009

GENRES

Heavy metal, hard rock

ONLY THE
GOOD DIE YOUNG

RANDY RHOADS

ROCK INNOVATOR WITH CLASSICAL LEANINGS

After being fired by Black Sabbath, Ozzy Osbourne's early success in his solo career was due in no small measure to his guitarist and co-writer, Randy Rhoads. A major influence on the neo-classical genre of metal, Rhoads is reckoned as one of the best rock guitarists of all time.

Born in Santa Monica, California, Randall William Rhoads' mother owned a music school, at which Rhoads himself taught. He was given his first guitar (classical) at the age of six, and his mother insisted on his also learning the piano and the elements of music theory.

QUIET RIOT

Rhoads quickly moved on to electric guitar, studying with a teacher at his mother's school. The family did not have a hi-fi in the house, and this enabled Rhoads to find his own style before being exposed to rock music. His first rock concert, Alice Cooper in 1971, was a revelation, opening his eyes to the full possibilities of the genre.

Quitting school to begin teaching at his mother's music school at the age of 16, Rhoads became a very popular teacher, and began playing in a range of bands with best friend, Kelly Garni, who played bass. The pair formed Quiet Riot in 1975, with Kevin DuBrow on vocals and Chris Forsyth on drums. They quickly gained a reputation on the LA music scene, often opening for Van Halen, but despite securing a record deal in Japan with CBS, and releasing two albums – *Quiet Riot* (1977) and *Quiet Riot II* (1978) (available in the US only as imports) – they were unable to secure either

a US deal or any kind of nationwide tour. So when Rhoads was asked to audition for Ozzy Osbourne, he did not need much encouragement. The audition was a success and Rhoads left for the UK in November 1979.

BLIZZARD OF OZZ

The band wasted no time recording their debut, releasing *Blizzard Of Ozz* in the UK in September 1980 (although it was not released in the States until 1981), and following it up with *Diary Of A Madman* (1981). Osbourne and Rhoads, so different in temperament, seemed to complement each other perfectly in the studio and on tour, with Rhoads' knowledge of music theory helping Osbourne to develop his more intuitive musical sense, and Osbourne happy to give Rhoads the freedom to explore his ideas.

Despite the success of the collaboration with Osbourne, Rhoads was uncomfortable with the rock–star label, preferring to view himself as just part of the band. His stellar live performances made this difficult, however, and he was already beginning to be viewed as a guitar icon. During the tour for *Diary Of A Madman*, Rhoads expressed his interest in studying for a degree in classical guitar, and would search out classical guitar teachers in each town they visited. Sadly, the world never got to see the fruits of this return to his roots. When the pilot of the plane Rhoads was travelling in tried to 'buzz' the tour bus and misjudged the approach, the plane crashed into a nearby property, instantly killing all on board.

DATE OF BIRTH

6 December 1956

DATE OF DEATH

19 March 1982

GENRES

Heavy metal, hard rock

MINNIE RIPERTON

LOVING HER IS EASY

Renowned for her extraordinary vocal range, and best known for her single 'Loving You' (1974), Minnie Riperton also brought a remarkable emotional intensity to her solo work, as well as providing backing vocals for a wide range of artists.

Riperton was born in Chicago, and started out in dance, although her vocal abilities were such that she trained briefly for a career in opera. Fortunately for the world of popular music, her interests led her in other directions. She started out singing with The Gems when she was 15, and the group signed to the legendary Chess label, releasing 'I Can't Help Myself' (1964) and 'He Makes Me Feel So Good' (1965). They became a session group called The Studio Three, providing backing vocals to a range of artists, but also continued to release their own records under various names, with 'My Baby's Real' (1967, released under the name The Starlets) achieving cult status in the northern soul scene.

EARLY CAREER

Riperton released a brace of solo singles under the name Andrea Davis – 'Lonely Girl' (1966) and 'You Gave Me Soul' (1967) – and joined the psychedelic soul band Rotary Connection, who released their eponymous debut album in 1967 and went on to release five more albums before breaking up in 1967. Among aficionados, Rotary Connection are highly rated but never achieved mainstream success.

The same combination of artistic excellence and lack of commercial success threatened to characterize Riperton's solo career. Her debut solo album, *Come To My Garden* (1970), is now widely considered a soul classic, but at the time it did

not sell well. She was a housewife and mother living in semi-retirement from the music business when she signed with Epic Records in 1973. Relocating to Los Angeles, she toured as a member of Stevie Wonder's backing band, and released her own album *Perfect Angel* in 1974, co-produced by Wonder.

LOVING YOU

Three singles were released from *Perfect Angel* before 'Loving You' (1975), the song that made her a household name. It was a massive hit, and both the single and its parent album achieved gold status. Her next solo work was *Adventures In Paradise* (1975), and then *Stay In Love* (1977), but neither of these releases matched the success of *Perfect Angel*. She continued to collaborate with Wonder, singing backing vocals on 'Ordinary Pain' from Wonder's masterpiece *Songs In The Key Of Life* (1976).

Minnie (1979) was the last album she released during her lifetime. In 1976, she was diagnosed with breast cancer and underwent a mastectomy. The cancer had already spread to her lymphatic system, however, and she was given six months to live. Fortunately, she had more time than that, and was able to continue recording and touring throughout 1977 and 1978, also becoming the national spokeswoman for the American Cancer Society and helping to raise awareness of what was still at that time a largely unspoken-about illness. By midway through 1979, though, she was confined to bed and she died in hospital on 12 July in her husband's arms. She was 31.

DATE OF BIRTH

8 November 1947

DATE OF DEATH

12 July 1979

GENRES

Soul, R&B

ONLY THE
GOOD DIE YOUNG

CHUCK SCHULDINER

GUITARIST AND FOUNDER OF METAL BAND DEATH

After taking lessons in classical guitar for less than a year, Charles Michael 'Chuck' Schuldiner immediately took to the electric guitar his parents bought him. Originally inspired by bands from the new wave of British heavy metal (NWOBHM), Schuldiner formed Mantas in 1983 and, after dissolving that band, founded Death in 1984.

1985's *Infernal Death* established Death's underground reputation, and the 1987 debut album, *Scream Bloody Gore*, is widely considered to be the defining death metal recording. Continuous and extensive line-up changes over the coming years, through which Schuldiner was the only constant, did not prevent the band continuing to release seminal albums, such as *Spiritual Healing* (1989) and *Human* (1991). The music developed considerably over time and the lyrics became more socially engaged, culminating in 1998's *The Sound Of Perseverance*, but when Schuldiner began to seek to express his more mainstream heavy metal songwriting ideas, he formed a new band, Control Denied, which released *The Fragile Art Of Existence* in 1999. Schuldiner was diagnosed with a malignant brain-stem tumour and underwent surgery in early 2000, finally succumbing to cancer at the end of 2001.

DATE OF BIRTH

13 May 1967

DATE OF DEATH

13 December 2001

GENRES

Death metal

INGO SCHWICHTENBERG

POWER METAL DRUMMER

Ingo Schwichtenberg (pictured second from the left), nicknamed 'Mr Smile', was famous for his high-energy drumming with German heavy metal band Helloween. He played on their recorded output from the 1985 EP *Helloween* and their debut full-length album *Walls Of Jericho* from the same year up to 1993's *Chameleon*, helping the band develop the genre of power metal by setting the drumming blueprint for other power metal players to follow.

The power metal genre appeared on 1987's *Keeper Of The Seven Keys Part 1* and was developed on the follow-up, *Keeper Of The Seven Keys Part 2* (1988). Their musical direction changed somewhat with *Pink Bubbles Go Ape* (1991), and by *Chameleon* in 1993, they had largely abandoned the power metal they did so much to create.

It was while touring *Chameleon* that both vocalist Michael Kiske and Schwichtenberg were fired, the latter for his dependence on drugs and alcohol as well as his worsening schizophrenia. Schwichtenberg was also reportedly unhappy with the musical direction of the band. After he left Helloween, Schwichtenberg's schizophrenia worsened, and he committed suicide in 1995 by jumping in front of a subway train.

DATE OF BIRTH

18 May 1965

DATE OF DEATH

8 March 1995

GENRES

Heavy metal

ONLY THE
GOOD DIE YOUNG

BON SCOTT

THE VOICE OF EARLY AC/DC

For many, AC/DC is the archetypal rock band, hard living and hard rocking, and it was the pairing of Angus Young's crunching guitar and the powerful vocals of Bon Scott that propelled them to that status. Singing about girls, booze and good times, Scott led the band to international success far beyond their native Australia.

Ronald Belford Scott was born in Forfar, Scotland, before moving to Melbourne, Australia, at the age of six. (The Young brothers, Angus and Malcolm, were also born in Scotland.) It was while at school in Melbourne that he acquired his nickname 'Bon', since he had recently arrived from Bonnie Scotland. Scott moved with his family to Fremantle, Australia, in 1956, where he dropped out of school and spent some time in a juvenile detention centre.

THE FORMATION OF AC/DC

Scott was the drummer with his first band, before becoming a singer with The Valentines, who achieved some success with their single 'Juliette' (1970). A move to Adelaide led to Scott joining Fraternity, who released two albums, *Livestock* (1971) and *Flaming Galah* (1972), and toured the UK in 1971.

But Scott still had some more dues to pay before true success came knocking. After Fraternity took a break in 1973, he spent some time working at the Wallaroo fertilizer plant, and singing with The Mount Lofty Rangers, where he began to develop his songwriting. A serious motorcycle accident nearly ended his story in 1974, but it was whilst recuperating

ONLY THE
GOOD DIE YOUNG

that he was introduced to AC/DC, a glam band from Sydney. After seeing them play, Scott thought that they were too young and inexperienced, and the band thought he was too old. Happily for rock history, they nevertheless got together for a jam, at the end of which Scott gained his place in the band.

LET THERE BE ROCK

Scott's first outings with AC/DC, *High Voltage* (1974) and *T.N.T.* (1975) were Australia-only releases (although a compilation of the two albums, *High Voltage* (1976), was released internationally). *Dirty Deeds Done Dirt Cheap* (1976) and *Let There Be Rock* (1977) also appeared in different versions in Australia and internationally, testifying to the fact that AC/DC had not yet become a major international act.

Powerage (1978) eventually went platinum in the US, but it was *Highway To Hell* (1979) that first broke into the US top 100 and firmly established AC/DC at the top of the international hard rock scene. Produced by Mutt Lange, the album shows the classic AC/DC sound fully in place, and sets the scene for the domination they were to achieve with their next release, *Back In Black* (1980). Sadly, Scott would not be part of it. In February 1980, after spending a night drinking heavily and sleeping in the car of an acquaintance, Scott was found dead from alcohol poisoning. With replacement singer Brian Johnson, *Back In Black* went on to become one of the best-selling albums of all time.

DATE OF BIRTH

9 July 1946

DATE OF DEATH

19 February 1980

GENRES

Hard rock, heavy metal

ONLY THE
GOOD DIE YOUNG

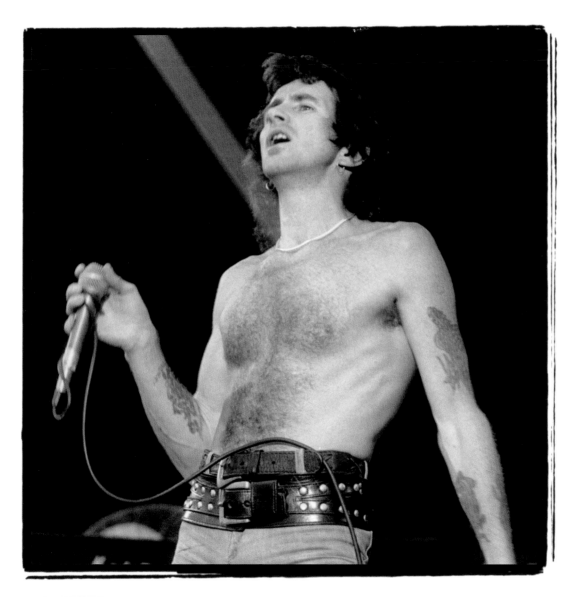

SELENA

TEJANO QUEEN

Born in Lake Jackson, Texas, Selena Quintanilla–Peréz began singing at the age of three, and by age nine was performing with the family singing group Selena Y Los Dinos, the band with which she performed until her death. She recorded her first album in 1985 (re-released in 1995 as *Mis Primeras Grabaciones*) and, despite not yet having a recording contract, she released six more albums over the next three years.

Quintanilla–Peréz was signed to Capitol/EMI in 1989, and 1990's *Ven Conmigo* went gold, the first tejano album by a female artist to do so. The early 1990s saw her career go from strength to strength, with a Grammy award for *Selena Live!* (1993) and a Grammy nomination for *Amor Prohibido* (1994), the latter spawning four No. 1 hits in the *Billboard* Latin Charts. She also began to move into fashion, opening two boutiques in 1994. Quintanilla–Peréz was shot in the early hours of 31 March 1995 by the former president of her fan club and boutique manager Yolanda Saldivar.

DATE OF BIRTH

16 April 1971

DATE OF DEATH

31 March 1995

GENRES

Latin pop

ONLY THE
GOOD DIE YOUNG

TUPAC SHAKUR
HiP-HOP PiONEER

Whilst he gained notoriety during his life for his often explicit and violent lyrics, not to mention his run-ins with the law, on his death Shakur left a substantial body of work, including numerous hit albums and many film appearances. He was undoubtedly one of the most influential and innovative figures in 1990s hip-hop. In 2010, his song 'Dear Mama' was added to the National Registry of the Library of Congress, testifying to his wider cultural significance.

Tupac Amaru Shakur was born in East Harlem, New York City, named after an eighteenth-century Peruvian revolutionary. Both his mother and father were members of the Black Panther Party, and he retained an active interest in political thought throughout his life. He had shown an interest in acting since the age of 12, but it was his rapping abilities that led him to a career in the entertainment industry when in 1990, by then based in Marin City, California, he became involved with the rap group Digital Underground.

SOLO SUCCESS

His rap debut was with 'Same Song', which was the lead track on Digital Underground's *This Is An EP Release* (1991), and he also appeared on their album *Sons Of The P* (1991). He began his solo career with *2Pacalypse Now* (1991), his most overtly political work, following it up with *Strictly 4 My N.I.G.G.A.Z.* (1993). But it was with his third album, *Me Against The World* (1995), that he achieved his commercial breakthrough, although the success of that pales in comparison with *All Eyez On Me* (1995), which achieved quintuple platinum status in just two months, and has now sold over 9 million copies. This would prove to be the last solo album released in his lifetime, although there have been six posthumous releases.

ONLY THE
GOOD DiE YOUNG

Shakur became increasingly notorious for his problems with the law. He was shot in November 1994, receiving five bullet wounds. The very next day he was in court to be convicted on three counts of molestation, for which he was sentenced in February 1995 to one-and-a-half to four-and-a-half years in prison. Shakur later accused Sean Combs and Biggie Smalls of involvement in the shooting, and also suspected his associate Randy 'Stretch' Walker of involvement.

THE RAP WARS RAGE ON

Shakur's incarceration meant that, with the release of *Me Against The World*, he was the first recording artist to have a No. 1 record while in jail. Suge Knight of Death Row Records posted bail of $1.4 million to secure his release in October 1995, in return for a three-album commitment, an investment that paid off handsomely following the success of *All Eyez On Me*, and subsequent posthumous releases.

At approximately 11.15 pm on 7 September 1996, Shakur was shot in a drive-by shooting in Las Vegas, dying in hospital six days later, one victim of the east coast–west coast rap wars that also claimed the life of Biggie Smalls.

DATE OF BIRTH

16 June 1971

DATE OF DEATH

13 September 1996

GENRES

Hip-hop

ONLY THE
GOOD DIE YOUNG

HILLEL SLOVAK

DISTINCTIVE FUNK GUITARIST

The hard-edged funk sound of The Red Hot Chili Peppers owed much to the guitar style of Hillel Slovak (pictured on the far right). Even after his death, Slovak's influence on the band was felt through his replacement, John Frusciante, a long-term fan of the band and Slovak's playing style in particular.

Slovak was born in Haifa, Israel, and emigrated with his family to the US when he was five. The family settled in Queens, New York, for a short while before moving to southern California. His first guitar was a bar mitzvah present, and he was heavily influenced by Jimi Hendrix and Led Zeppelin while learning to play.

THE EARLY DAYS

Slovak met Michael Balzary (aka Flea) and Jack Irons while at school. Slovak formed Anthym with Irons and two others, and it was after one of their early gigs that Slovak met Anthony Kiedis. It was Slovak that taught Balzary to play bass when the band's original bass player did not work out and, after graduating from high school, the band changed its name to What Is This?, although Balzary left shortly after this to play with Fear.

The trio of Slovak, Kiedis and Balzary continued to make their own music, however, forming a side project with Irons, originally called Tony Flow & The Miraculously Majestic Masters Of Mayhem. It was not intended to be a long-term project, but they kept on being asked back whenever they played and they worked on extending their repertoire, eventually changing their name to The Red Hot Chili Peppers. They recorded a demo and managed to secure a deal with EMI, with Balzary leaving Fear to concentrate on the band.

At the same time, however, What Is This? also secured a record deal, and Slovak left The Chili Peppers, which he still considered essentially a side-project. His time with What Is This? yielded two EPs (*Squeezed*, 1984 and *3 Out Of 5 Live*, 1985) and an album, 1985's *What Is This*, but Slovak became dissatisfied with the band. In the meantime, The Red Hot Chili Peppers had recorded and released their debut album. Hillel returned to the fold for the band's second album, *Freaky Styley* (1985) and, after a spell in rehab, participated in the recording of *The Uplift Mofo Party Plan* (1987).

RECORDING AND ADDICTION

Both Slovak and Kiedis were addicted to heroin, but it was Kiedis' addiction that seemed the more problematic. Both agreed to stop using before embarking on the promotional tour for *The Uplift Mofo Party Plan*. It was Slovak, however, who found this more difficult, and he missed several shows with the band. On returning, he isolated himself from the rest of the band, and when they were unable to get in touch with him, the police found him dead in his Hollywood apartment. His last recording, 'Fire', appeared posthumously on *The Abbey Road EP* (1988) and *Mother's Milk* (1989), but his lasting influence was the pivotal role he played in defining the band's hard-edged funky sound.

DATE OF BIRTH

13 April 1962

DATE OF DEATH

25 June 1988

GENRES

Funk rock, alternative rock

ONLY THE
GOOD DIE YOUNG

ELLIOTT SMITH

SINGER-SONGWRITER AND MULTI-INSTRUMENTALIST

Steven Paul Smith (who began calling himself Elliott after high school) began playing piano at the age of nine and guitar at 10. After moving from Texas to Portland, Oregon, at 14, he formed Heatmiser whilst at college.

Heatmiser released two albums and an EP on Frontier Records in 1993–94, before signing to Virgin and releasing *Mic City Sons* in 1996. However, by then the band had split up due to Smith's increasingly successful solo career, which began with 1994's *Roman Candle*. After two further solo albums, Smith contributed material to the soundtrack of *Good Will Hunting* (1997), from which the song 'Miss Misery' was nominated for an Academy Award.

After 1998, Smith fell into depression. Two further albums were produced (*XO*, 1998 and *Figure 8*, 2000), before heroin addiction and increasing paranoia led to a series of unfinished projects and poor live performances. Ironically, by the time of his death (which many do not accept as suicide), he had been clean for up to a year. The album he had been working on, *From A Basement On A Hill*, was released posthumously in 2004.

DATE OF BIRTH

6 August 1969

DATE OF DEATH

21 October 2003

GENRES

Indie rock

ONLY THE
GOOD DIE YOUNG

LAYNE STALEY

RECLUSIVE ROCK VOCALIST

Alice In Chains frontman Layne Staley sat dead in his apartment for two weeks before he was discovered, surrounded by drugs paraphernalia. Such a sad end should not distract, however, from his extraordinary achievements.

Born in Kirkland, Washington, he began playing drums at the age of 12, playing in several glam bands, but he began to harbour aspirations to become a singer. It was while singing with Alice N' Chains, a speed metal band which played the Seattle area in the mid-1980s, that Staley met future Alice In Chains guitarist Jerry Cantrell, and the pair lived together for a while in a dilapidated rehearsal space. By 1987, Staley had joined Cantrell's band, which adopted the name Alice In Chains.

PLATINUM SUCCESS

Staley can take credit for the majority of the band's lyrics, but the incredible success of Alice In Chains occurred almost in spite of him. Once they released their debut album, *Facelift*, in 1990, success came quickly. The second single from the album, 'Man in the Box', was an enormous hit, and the album went double platinum. The follow-up album, *Dirt* (1992), was an even bigger success, certified as quadruple platinum. But whilst the band had done a two-year tour of their debut release, they could not do the same for its successor, due to Staley's drug addiction.

Despite also being unable to tour in support of their 1994 acoustic EP, *Jar of Flies*, it still went straight to No. 1. A short spell in rehab having little discernible effect on Staley's drug-taking, he began work on a side-project, Mad Season,

which featured Mike McCready of Pearl Jam and Barrett Martin of Screaming Trees. The band released one album, *Above* (1995), and two singles were moderately successful. When Alice In Chains released their third album, *Alice In Chains* (1995), it too went double platinum, despite once again the band not being able to tour much in support of the release.

RECLUSE

Staley made his last appearance with the band on 3 July 1996, and in October of that year, Staley's ex-girlfriend, Demri Lara Parrott, died from complications caused by her drug use. Her death had a profound effect on Staley, and from that time his addiction and depression worsened considerably.

Despite recording two tracks, 'Get Born Again' and 'Died', with Alice in Chains in 1998, released on the box set *Music Bank* (1999), and recording some vocal tracks for Class of '99 in November 1998, for all intents and purposes Staley was now a recluse. The success of his recordings had given him the ability to live the addict's life without worrying about money, and the fact that dealers were prepared to deliver to his door allowed him to retreat into an empty and solitary existence. When his body was found on 19 April 2002, after his accountant had informed his mother that no money had been withdrawn from his account for two weeks, police also found a stash of cocaine, two loaded crack pipes, and one full and several used syringes.

DATE OF BIRTH

22 August 1967

DATE OF DEATH

5 April 2002

GENRES

Alt metal, grunge, alternative rock, heavy metal

RORY STORM

LEADING LIGHT OF THE MERSEY BEAT SCENE

Born Alan Caldwell, Rory Storm (pictured on the far left) was active in the skiffle scene in Liverpool in the late 1950s before forming Rory Storm & The Hurricanes in 1959. The band featured one Richard Starkie on drums, soon to change his name to Ringo Starr.

In October 1960, the band travelled to Hamburg, playing at the Kaiserkeller, alternating sets with The Beatles. It was while both groups were in Hamburg that Lennon, McCartney, Harrison and Starr recorded together for the first time, backing The Hurricanes' bassist/vocalist Lu Walters.

Rory Storm & The Hurricanes continued to play as a band after Starr's departure for The Beatles in August 1962, and the two bands often shared the same bill. Rory Storm was an extravagant performer, but his insistence on continuing to perform covers and the fact that the band released only two singles meant that they never achieved wider success. After The Hurricanes were disbanded in 1967, Storm became a DJ, before dying at his home in Liverpool in 1972 from an overdose of sleeping tablets, on the same night as his mother.

DATE OF BIRTH

21 September 1939

DATE OF DEATH

28 September 1972

GENRES

Skiffle

ONLY THE
GOOD DIE YOUNG

STUART SUTCLIFFE

THE PRE-EMINENT 'FIFTH BEATLE'

One of many people to enjoy the sobriquet 'the fifth Beatle', Sutcliffe has a better claim to this title than most. Far more accomplished as an artist than a musician, it is nevertheless his short involvement with The Beatles that has led to his lasting fame.

Sutcliffe was born in Edinburgh, but brought up in Liverpool. He was introduced to John Lennon while both were studying at Liverpool College of Art, and the two shared a flat. Sutcliffe was already showing great talent as a painter, and managed to sell one of his paintings for £65. Lennon persuaded him to use this windfall to buy a bass guitar and join Lennon's band.

WITH THE BEATLES

It is impossible to verify Sutcliffe's ability on his chosen instrument. A rehearsal tape from 1960, three tracks from which found their way onto The Beatles *Anthology 1* (1995), provides no clear evidence. Sutcliffe had some background in music, having had piano lessons since the age of nine, but George Harrison later recalled that 'Stu had no idea how to play'.

Nevertheless, the band must have been doing something right. After The Beatles, as they had by this stage become, played at his Jacaranda club, Allan Williams became their promoter, and he offered the band bookings in Hamburg (albeit only after Rory Storm & The Hurricanes and Gerry & The Pacemakers had both turned him down).

The band started off playing at the Indra and then moved to the Kaiserkeller, both located on the Grosse Freiheit, right in the centre of Hamburg's red-light district. Living conditions were primitive, and they had to play four sets every night, seven nights a week. Sutcliffe began wearing sunglasses and tight leather trousers, and his performance of 'Love Me Tender' became one of the highlights of their set. When they moved to the Top Ten club, the owner of the Kaiserkeller reported Harrison for working under the legal age limit and he was deported. Best and McCartney were also deported on 4 December, and Lennon left a few days later. Sutcliffe and the other Beatles returned to Hamburg in March to resume their residency at the Top Ten club, although he decided to leave the band in July of that year to concentrate on his painting.

ASTRID AND ART

Right from the beginning, there were those who were worried that Sutcliffe's involvement with The Beatles would distract him from his art, and, given his rudimentary bass playing, it is little surprise that Sutcliffe returned to painting, for which he had a genuine talent. He had been dating Astrid Kirchherr, a photographer, in Hamburg, and they were engaged in November 1960. It was Kirchherr who invented the mop-top haircut, with Sutcliffe being the first in the group to sport it. After leaving The Beatles, Sutcliffe attended the Hamburg College of Art. During this period, Sutcliffe began suffering from intense headaches, but doctors in Germany and England were unable to find anything wrong. He died from a brain haemorrhage in an ambulance on the way to hospital after collapsing on 10 April 1962.

DATE OF BIRTH

23 June 1940

DATE OF DEATH

10 April 1962

GENRES

Rock, pop

ONLY THE
GOOD DIE YOUNG

TAMMI TERRELL

SOUL DIVA

One of the greatest female singers to come from Motown's illustrious stable, Terrell's exquisite melodic sense put her in a class above most of the competition. Despite being most famous for her work with Marvin Gaye from the late 1960s, Terrell (born Thomasina Winifred Montgomery) had already enjoyed a varied career before releasing the duets that made her name.

Born in Philadelphia, she changed her name from Thomasina to Tammy in 1957. It was around this time that she first began complaining of the headaches that would plague her throughout her life. This did not prevent her beginning her professional singing career at the age of 13, opening club dates for Gary 'US' Bonds and Patti LaBelle & The Blue Belles, amongst others. In 1960, still not 15, she signed to Scepter Records, releasing two singles – 'If You See Bill' (1961) and 'Voice of Experience' (1962) – released on Scepter subsidiary Wand Records), still under the name Tammy Montgomery.

RISING STAR

She joined James Brown's Revue, releasing 'I Cried' (1963) on Brown's Try Me Records. She was romantically involved with Brown, but Brown's violence towards her led to the end of their association in 1964. A duet with Jimmy Radcliffe, 'If I Would Marry You' (1964), was recorded for Checker Records, but Terrell then enrolled at the University of Pennsylvania. Terrell did not let her studies prevent her performing entirely, however, and after being spotted in Detroit by Berry Gordy she signed to Motown Records.

ONLY THE
GOOD DIE YOUNG

With Gordy changing her name to Tammi Terrell, her debut release for Motown was 'I Can't Believe You Love Me' (1965). This and subsequent singles were successful enough to land her a spot on the Motortown Revue. But it was when she was paired with Marvin Gaye in 1967 that she truly found the setting in which her talent could shine.

TAMMI AND MARVIN

Terrell and Gaye were never lovers, and indeed many of their duets were not even recorded as duets, but instead created by overdubbing. But they did become close friends, and had a mutual respect for each other's musicality, and it is beyond doubt that the three albums of duets that they committed to vinyl – *United* (1967), *You're All I Need* (1968) and *Easy* (1969) – exude a rare chemistry.

On 14 October 1967, during what was to become her last live performance, Terrell collapsed. She was rushed to hospital where she was diagnosed with a malignant brain tumour. It was while undergoing eight operations, and with her health in decline, that the second two albums were recorded. It is disputed to what degree she appears on the third album at all, with Gaye maintaining that the female vocals were sung by Valerie Simpson. Simpson herself says that although she sang guide vocals, it is Terrell that is heard on the final result.

A solo album, *Irresistible* (1969), was released by Motown shortly before her death. In January 1970, she underwent her final operation, after which she lapsed into a coma, dying on 16 March, a month and a half short of her 25th birthday.

DATE OF BIRTH

29 April 1945

DATE OF DEATH

16 March 1970

GENRES

R&B, soul, pop

ONLY THE
GOOD DIE YOUNG

GARY THAIN

INTENSE AND MELODIC BASS PLAYER

New Zealand–born Gary Thain (pictured second from the right) is best known for his work with Uriah Heep, but he had already had some measure of success. He moved to the UK in 1966, playing with several bands (and allegedly once jamming with Jimi Hendrix) before joining The Keef Hartley Band, playing on six of their albums and appearing at Woodstock. In 1970, he recorded 'Fiends and Angels' with Martha Velez, with Eric Clapton and Christine McVie also on the session.

The Keef Hartley Band dissolved in 1972 and Thain joined Uriah Heep, playing his first gig with them on 1 February at the Whisky a Go Go in Los Angeles. He appeared with the band on five albums between 1972 and 1974, beginning with *Demons And Wizards* (1972) just four months after joining the band.

His distinctive and intense playing style, using his thumb rather than a plectrum, and his songwriting abilities contributed much to Uriah Heep, although his increasing use of drink and drugs led to him leaving the band in January 1972. By the end of the year he was dead from a drugs overdose.

DATE OF BIRTH

15 May 1948

DATE OF DEATH

8 December 1975

GENRES

Hard rock, prog rock, heavy metal

ONLY THE
GOOD DIE YOUNG

RICHARD TURNER

VERSATILE JAZZ TRUMPETER AND PROMOTER

Born and raised in Leeds, Richard Turner (pictured in the background) was the son of a classical saxophonist and a music teacher. At 16, he enrolled at Leeds College of Music, and later moved to the Royal Academy of Music where he was a student on their jazz course.

He played in the jazz–fusion band Drive, and contributed to the live shows of Mercury Music Prize–nominated band Friendly Fires, but it was in his own quartet, Round Trip, that the influence of such jazz greats as Clifford Brown and Clark Terry was most apparent. Round Trip released their eponymously titled debut album in April 2011, featuring Turner's own compositions, and Turner was preparing material for its follow–up at the time of his death.

Turner was also a jazz promoter, from October 2006 running the Con Cellar jazz bar in Camden, London, which soon became a meeting place for best of the new crop of British jazz players. In addition, Turner was a competition–standard swimmer. It was while swimming at a pool in south London that he died of a ruptured aortic aneurysm.

DATE OF BIRTH

30 July 1984

DATE OF DEATH

11 August 2011

GENRES

Indie rock, pop, disco, contemporary jazz

RITCHIE VALENS

LATINO ROCK'N'ROLL PIONEER

In a recording career that lasted under a year, Ritchie Valens managed to encapsulate the teenage energy of rock'n'roll and become a wildly popular Spanish-speaking pioneer of the youthful music.

Born Richard Steven Valenzuela in Pacoima, California, he was immersed from a young age in mariachi as well as R&B. He learnt trumpet and drums as well as the guitar, which he played in the conventional manner despite being left-handed. At the age of 16 he joined The Silhouettes, becoming the lead vocalist as well as the guitarist. The band quickly became local stars.

RECORDING CAREER

The Silhouettes came to the attention of Bob Keane, the owner of Del-Fi Records. Valens auditioned at Keane's house in Los Angeles, where he had a small studio in his basement. The recordings made that day were later released on the album *Ritchie Valens: The Lost Tapes* (1995), and although they were never intended for public consumption when they were made, Valens' talent still shines through.

Keane played a pivotal role in Valens' short career, deciding that he ought to shorten his name, and booking him into Gold Star Studios with a backing band. The songs 'Come On, Let's Go' and the Lieber and Stoller tune 'Framed' were recorded at the first session in summer 1958, and the record appeared as *Billboard* magazine's 'pick of the week' on 1 September. A double A-side, 'Donna' and 'La Bamba', followed shortly after. It is astounding to think that these were the only records released in Valens' lifetime.

ONLY THE
GOOD DIE YOUNG

Keane capitalized on the success of these records by booking gigs all across the United States. Valens dropped out of high school and travelled up and down the east coast in October 1958, appearing on *Dick Clark's American Bandstand*, and then playing at the Honolulu Civic Auditorium in November. He returned to Los Angeles to play a homecoming concert at Pacoima Jr High School on 10 December (this concert appeared as an album in 1959). Mid-December saw him back on the east coast, appearing on *Alan Freed's Christmas Jubilee* and *Dick Clark's American Bandstand* for a second time. He played New York's Apollo Theatre early in 1959, before heading back west and appearing in the Alan Freed film *Go Johnny Go!* along with Chuck Berry. This film provides the only live footage of Valens in existence. Amongst this hectic schedule, he managed to find the time to record enough material for two albums, *Ritchie Valens* and *Ritchie*, both released posthumously in 1959.

THE FINAL TOUR

Valens joined the Winter Dance Party Concert tour, travelling with Buddy Holly, The Big Bopper, Waylon Jennings and others. They criss-crossed mid-west America in freezing temperatures on buses with inadequate heating. When, in February, Holly proposed chartering a plane, the idea was understandably popular. Valens tossed a coin with Jennings to decide who would get the last space, and when Jennings lost, he said jokingly, 'I hope your plane crashes'. Causing Jennings lifelong guilt, this is precisely what happened, the crash killing Valens, Holly, The Big Bopper and pilot Roger Peterson.

DATE OF BIRTH

13 May 1941

DATE OF DEATH

3 February 1959

GENRES

Rock'n'roll

ONLY THE
GOOD DIE YOUNG

RONNIE VAN ZANT

LEAD SINGER OF LYNYRD SKYNYRD

Van Zant was born in one of the toughest neighbourhoods of Jacksonville, Florida. Whilst baseball was an early passion, by 1965 he was playing with the musicians that formed the early core of Lynyrd Skynyrd.

The band had to go through several name changes before settling on Lynyrd Skynyrd (a back-handed tribute to a school gym teacher), and although they recorded a demo in 1970, which led to an offer of a contract with Capricorn records (which Van Zant turned down), it was not until 1973, after some personnel changes, that the band were signed by Sounds of the South, and recorded their debut album *Pronounced Leh-nerd Skin'nerd*, produced by Al Kooper. *Second Helping* (1974) contained their breakthrough hit, 'Sweet Home Alabama', and went multi-platinum. *Nuthin' Fancy* and *Gimme Back My Bullets* (both from 1975) did not sell as well as their predecessors, but continued to showcase the band's no-nonsense Southern rock. *Street Survivors* (1977) was released just three days before the plane crash that killed Van Zant and two other band members, and went platinum shortly after.

DATE OF BIRTH

15 January 1948

DATE OF DEATH

20 October 1977

GENRES

Southern rock

ONLY THE
GOOD DIE YOUNG

STEVIE RAY VAUGHAN
BLUES ROCK GUITAR MAESTRO

The blues is always with us, running like a golden thread through the history of rock music, but in its raw form its popularity waxes and wanes. With his stunning virtuosity and biting attack, Vaughan was the catalyst for the blues revival of the 1980s, building on and developing the work of the blues–rock guitarists of the late 1960s.

Born in Dallas, Texas, Vaughan's father bought him his first guitar when he was seven, and he soon became obsessed with the instrument, playing along to his older brother Jimmie's records, copying note for note the work of guitarists such as Buddy Guy, Muddy Waters and, perhaps most significantly, Jimi Hendrix. He began playing in various bands from the age of 12, and dropped out of school when he was 17 to concentrate on his music, moving to Austin, Texas with his first blues band, Blackbird, in 1971.

EARLY CAREER

Like any self–respecting blues musician, Vaughan paid his dues playing in a range of bands, making occasional recordings that never quite got released, even spending a period living in the Rolling Hills club, sleeping on the pool table or the floor.

The first band that Vaughan led was Triple Threat Revue, formed in 1977. By 1979, with the departure of vocalist Lou Ann Barton, the band changed its name to Double Trouble, and Vaughan took on lead vocalist duties. The band performed at the Montreux Jazz Festival in 1982, where the guitarist was asked by David Bowie to play on his next record, *Let's Dance* (1983). Although the record became Bowie's best-selling to date, perhaps more significant for

ONLY THE
GOOD DIE YOUNG

Vaughan's career was the record contract Double Trouble landed with Epic, which led to *Texas Flood*, recorded over two days at the end of 1982 and released in 1983. A critical success, Vaughan quickly followed it up with *Couldn't Stand The Weather* (1984), which by 1985 had gone gold, and *Soul To Soul* (1985).

SOBERING UP AND MOVING ON

The band's success led to Vaughan indulging in alcohol and drugs on a quite epic scale. It began to affect his music, with the *Live Alive* (1986) album falling short of his own high standards, although still containing moments of genius. He was hospitalized after collapsing in Germany in September 1986, and underwent drug rehabilitation in the States.

His new-found sobriety informed the recording of *In Step* (1989), which showed the band widening the range of their music beyond the blues, although when Vaughan went into the studio with his brother Jimmie, the resulting *Family Style*, recorded in early 1990 but not released until 1991, was firmly in blues territory, despite Nile Rodgers' glossy production.

Double Trouble opened for Eric Clapton for two shows in Wisconsin in August 1990. The encore of the second show featured a jam with Vaughan and his brother, Robert Cray, Buddy Guy and Clapton himself, a fitting encapsulation of the 1980s blues scene Vaughan had done so much to sustain. After the show, Vaughan boarded a helicopter bound for Chicago; it crashed into a hillside, killing everyone on board.

DATE OF BIRTH

3 October 1954

DATE OF DEATH

27 August 1990

GENRES

Blues, blues rock, Texas blues

ONLY THE
GOOD DIE YOUNG

SiD ViCiOUS

BASS PLAYER WiTH THE SEX PiSTOLS

John Simon Ritchie was born in Lewisham, south-east London, although he moved with his mother to Ibiza shortly after his birth, returning to London in 1961. Ritchie left school at the age of 15 and enrolled as Simon Beverley (taking his stepfather's name) in Hackney Technical College to study art.

It was here that he met John Lydon and first acquired the name under which he later found fame, 'Sid Vicious', after Lydon's pet hamster. By the age of 17, he was living in a squat, occasionally busking with Lydon, and began spending time at a shop on the Kings Road managed by Malcolm McLaren. It is during this period that The Sex Pistols were formed. Some say that Vicious was mentioned as a possible singer, but his friend Lydon beat him to it. Vicious got his first taste of live performance during the first-ever punk festival at the 100 Club in September 1976 drumming for Siouxsie & The Banshees. Headlining the festival were, of course, The Sex Pistols.

THE SEX PiSTOLS

Vicious was one of The Sex Pistols' most loyal fans, and after Glen Matlock left the band in January 1977, Vicious replaced him. His bass playing was rudimentary at best, and most of the bass on *Never Mind The Bollocks* (1977) was played by Steve Jones, although Vicious managed to make it onto one track, 'Bodies'.

The band had already been signed and dropped by A&M (and EMI before them) by the time of Vicious' live debut with the band on 3 April 1977, signing with Virgin on 12 May. Their single 'God Save The Queen' was banned,

ONLY THE
GOOD DiE YOUNG

but it still sold enough copies to reach No. 1, although this was not officially recognized. The band's increasing notoriety meant that they had to tour under various pseudonyms. Their last gig in England was at a miners benefit in Huddersfield in December 1977. The band then left for an ill-fated American tour in January 1978, at the final gig of which in San Francisco the band finally split.

SID AND NANCY

Vicious had been seeing Nancy Spungen since early 1977. A self-confessed junkie and groupie, Spungen had arrived in the UK with the express intent of bedding a Sex Pistol, and the couple had become locked in a destructive cycle of heavy drug use, which only worsened when the band broke up. After a short spell in London, the couple returned to America and moved into New York's Chelsea Hotel.

Nancy managed to arrange a few gigs for Vicious, and he was paid some royalties by McLaren. But Vicious awoke on 12 October 1978 to find Spungen dead in the bathroom with a stab wound to her abdomen, and he was arrested and charged with murder. He was released on bail (the $50,000 being raised by Virgin), but soon found himself back inside after being involved in a fight. Released once more on bail on 1 February 1979, Vicious overdosed at a party on heroin supplied by his mother and by the morning was dead.

DATE OF BIRTH

10 May 1957

DATE OF DEATH

2 February 1979

GENRES

Punk rock

ONLY THE
GOOD DIE YOUNG

CHUCK WAGON

MULTI-INSTRUMENTALIST MEMBER OF THE DICKIES

Robert Davis, known by his stage name Chuck Wagon (pictured on the far right), was a member of The Dickies' original line-up that began playing around the LA punk scene in 1977. Davis played guitar, keyboards, harmonica, saxophone and drums, and can be heard on four tracks on the album *Stukas Over Disneyland* (1983), released after his death.

Known for their outlandish stage shows, featuring strange costumes, puppets and a midget roadie, they became the first LA punk band to secure a major label record deal, signing with A&M in 1978. Their debut single from the same year featured a cover of Black Sabbath's 'Paranoid' as well as original songs 'Hideous' and 'You Drive Me Ape (You Big Gorilla)'. Their debut album, *The Incredible Shrinking Dickies* (1979), spawned the UK hit 'Banana Splits (Tra La La Song)'. *Dawn Of The Dickies*, from later the same year, followed the same template.

Davis quit the band in early 1981, but was persuaded to return for some live shows. He shot himself in the head after a gig on 27 June 1981, and died in hospital the next morning.

DATE OF BIRTH

11 August 1956

DATE OF DEATH

28 June 1981

GENRES

Punk rock

CLARENCE WHITE

BLUEGRASS AND COUNTRY ROCK INNOVATOR

Few guitarists achieve pre-eminence in one genre. Clarence White achieved pre-eminence in three, not only mastering acoustic bluegrass, electric country and rock guitar, but also expanding the possibilities of all three. Roger McGuinn from The Byrds called him the best musician he ever worked with.

White got an early start in music. After moving to Burbank, California, in 1954 the four White siblings, Roland, Eric Jr, Clarence and Joanne, formed their own band, the misleadingly titled Three Little Country Boys, although with Joanne's departure in 1955 the name became more appropriate. When Roland heard 'Pike Country Breakdown' by Bill Monroe, The Three Little Country Boys became a bluegrass band.

BLUEGRASS PRE-EMINENCE

The band changed their name to The Country Boys when banjo player Billy Ray Latham joined, and they recorded their first single in 1959. They appeared several times on the *Andy Griffith Show*, releasing two more singles. The existence of another set of Country Boys required a name change, and they released their debut album, *The New Sounds Of Bluegrass America* (1962), as the Kentucky Colonels. White began to develop his guitar as a lead instrument after seeing Doc Watson, and this new style was demonstrated on *New Dimensions In Banjo And Bluegrass* (1963), which he recorded with banjo players Eric Weissberg and Marshall Brickman, and which became far better known when it was reissued, with the addition of 'Duelling Banjos', as the soundtrack to the film *Deliverance* (1973).

The Kentucky Colonels' 1964 outing, *Appalachian Swing*, is a landmark in the development of bluegrass, but the band found it harder and harder to make a living playing the music they loved, and finally disbanded in October 1965.

ELECTRIFIED

Instead of being disheartened, White bought a '54 Fender Telecaster and began modifying his technique in order to get the most out of the instrument. Although he continued to play acoustic guitar, he worked more and more in an electric context, with Gene Parsons and Gib Guilbeau as Cajun Gib & Gene, and for a short period with a country group called Trio. But it was his involvement with The Byrds, first as a session musician and then as a fully fledged member of the group, that launched the next important phase of his career.

White played on all five studio albums that The Byrds released between 1969 and 1971, including *Ballad Of Easy Rider* (1969) and *[Untitled]* (1970) (the latter so-named because the studio mistook a note saying that the album had no title for the title itself). Although these records do not show him off to best effect, his skilful playing made this late-period incarnation of the band a powerful live act.

White continued to do session work whilst with The Byrds and, after the band dissolved in 1973, participated in Muleskinner, which released the progressive bluegrass album *Muleskinner* (1973). He also reunited with brothers Eric and Roland as the New Kentucky Colonels. It was while loading gear into a car after a Colonels gig in Palmdale, California, that White was hit and killed by a drunk driver.

DATE OF BIRTH

7 June 1944

DATE OF DEATH

15 June 1973

GENRES

Rock, bluegrass, country rock

ONLY THE
GOOD DIE YOUNG

DANNY WHITTEN

MEMBER OF CRAZY HORSE

Born in Columbus, Georgia, by 1967 Whitten had gravitated to San Francisco and was playing with The Rockets, who released a poorly selling, self-titled album on White Whale Records in 1968. But songwriter Neil Young began jamming with the group, and they soon became known as Crazy Horse.

Young's second solo album, *Everybody Knows This Is Nowhere* (1969), was credited to Neil Young & Crazy Horse, featuring Whitten on second guitar and vocals. Whitten performs on three tracks of Young's 1970 album *After The Gold Rush*, but his addiction to heroin led to him being dismissed halfway through the sessions.

Crazy Horse released their own debut album, *Crazy Horse*, in 1971. It contains Whitten's best-known song, 'I Don't Want To Talk About It', but Whitten's continued drug use led to him being dismissed from that band as well. He was recruited by Young to play guitar on the tour for the *Harvest* album. Young fired him on 18 November 1972, receiving a call that very same night informing him of Whitten's death from an overdose of Valium and alcohol.

DATE OF BIRTH

8 May 1943

DATE OF DEATH

18 November 1972

GENRES

Country rock, folk rock, hard rock

ONLY THE
GOOD DIE YOUNG

HANK WILLIAMS

THE MAN WHO INVENTED MODERN COUNTRY MUSIC

In a recording career lasting little over six years and consisting of only 35 singles (11 of which were No. 1 hits), Hank Williams managed single-handedly to redefine country music, his direct and emotional songs capturing the uncertainties of a world in transition after the Second World War.

Born Hiram King Williams in Mount Olive, Alabama, Williams began using the name Hank in 1937. By then he had already won the $15 first prize in a songwriting competition and begun to host his own show on the WSFA radio station in Montgomery, Alabama. He formed The Drifting Cowboys, but when the rest of his band were drafted into the US Army Williams' alcoholism made it difficult for him to recruit replacements, and in addition he was sacked from his radio show for persistent drunkenness.

RIDING HIGH

In September 1946, he auditioned for (and was rejected by) the *Grand Ole Opry*, but in December 1946 his first recording session earned him the attention of MGM Records, who signed him in 1947. That year, 'Move It On Over' became a country hit, but it was his 1949 version of the old Friend and Mills song 'Lovesick Blues' that provided him with truly massive success, earning him a place on the *Grand Ole Opry* that had rejected him just a few years before. He followed it up with seven more hit songs that year, including 'Mind Your Own Business' and 'You're Gonna Change (Or I'm Gonna Leave)'.

ONLY THE GOOD DIE YOUNG

In 1950, Williams also began recording as 'Luke the Drifter', a convenient vehicle for his more explicitly religious material, although the identity of the wandering and rather folksy Luke was never in doubt, with Williams often incorporating the material into his sets. And the hits recorded under his own name kept on coming: 'Long Gone Lonesome Blues', 'Why Don't You Love Me' and 'Moanin' The Blues' provided him with three No. 1s in the country charts in that year alone. 1951 continued in a similar vein. Tony Bennett's cover of 'Dear John', the B-side of 'Cold, Cold Heart', testified to the increasing recognition of his songwriting abilities beyond the country sphere.

THE END OF THE ROAD

But beyond the hits, 1951 proved to be the beginning of the end, with a fall during a hunting trip aggravating the back pain that had plagued him all this life (Williams was born with a mild form of spina bifida). This led him to drink even more heavily, in addition developing an addiction to morphine. Collaborators began to drift away, he was fired from the *Grand Ole Opry* in August 1952, and he divorced his wife of six years, Audrey. Whilst the hits kept on coming, and Williams kept on touring, his dependence on alcohol and drugs worsened, and he died in the back of a car being driven to a gig sometime after midnight on 1 January 1953. Despite the brevity of his recording career, the emotional directness of his songs and the compelling vulnerability of his delivery set country music forever on a new path.

DATE OF BIRTH

17 September 1923

DATE OF DEATH

1 January 1953

GENRES

Country

ALAN 'BLIND OWL' WILSON

SCHOLAR OF THE BLUES

Born in Boston, Massachusetts, Wilson studied music at Boston University. He was a frequent player on the Cambridge coffee house circuit and wrote two important articles on the blues for *Broadside* magazine, acquiring his nickname 'Blind Owl' due to his poor vision.

Wilson played harmonica and second guitar with Son House on the latter's *Father Of The Delta Blues* (1965), also appearing on *John The Revelator* (1970) (re-issued in 1995 as *Delta Blues And Spirituals*), recorded when House was playing at the 100 Club in London. Even Canned Heat – the innovative blues rock band who released their eponymous debut album in 1967, and with whom Wilson played until his death – often featured an older generation of blues legends on their records, including Sunnyland Slim on piano for 1968's *Boogie With Canned Heat*. Sunnyland Slim's own *Slim's Got His Thing Goin' On* (1968) featured Canned Heat as his backing band. 1970's double album *Hooker 'N Heat* featured the band and John Lee Hooker. It is unclear whether Wilson's death was a suicide or the result of an accidental overdose.

DATE OF BIRTH

4 July 1943

DATE OF DEATH

3 September 1970

GENRES

Blues rock

ONLY THE
GOOD DIE YOUNG

RICKY WILSON

DISTINCTIVE GUITARIST WITH THE B-52's

Ricky Wilson (pictured on the far left) was a founder member of The B-52's, the quirky Athens, Georgia-based new wave band. They played their first gig on Valentine's Day 1977, and released their first single 'Rock Lobster' in 1978. After signing to Warner Bros, their debut album *The B-52's* was released in 1979, eventually going platinum. The follow-up, *Wild Planet* (1980), went gold. Wilson also played guitar on one track on Tom Verlaine's debut solo album, *Tom Verlaine* (1979).

A collaboration between The B-52's and David Byrne in 1981 was abandoned, resulting in 1982's six-track EP *Mesopotamia* instead of the projected album, but 1983 saw another full-length album, *Whammy!*, the result of experimentation with drum machines and synthesizers. *Bouncing Off The Satellites* (1985) was the last of the band's records to feature Wilson, who succumbed to AIDS-related illness at the end of that year.

Wilson's guitar style was unique, usually playing with just four strings (and occasionally five), tuned to his own distinctive open tunings. This allowed him to play bass patterns on the lower strings and lead parts on the top strings.

DATE OF BIRTH

19 March 1953

DATE OF DEATH

12 October 1985

GENRES

New wave, post-punk, pop rock

ONLY THE
GOOD DIE YOUNG

AMY WINEHOUSE

SMOKEY-VOICED DIVA

For many years, Amy Winehouse's life was a tabloid editor's dream, with her drug, alcohol and marital problems played out in the world's media. But ultimately, even the most lurid tales cannot hide the sheer fact of her talent, tragically cut short by her early death.

Born in Southgate, north London, she grew up listening to the jazz records of her father, Mitch, and cited jazz singers such as Sarah Vaughn and Dinah Washington as her primary influences. She had a stage school education, attending the Sylvia Young Theatre School and the BRIT School among others. She signed to Simon Fuller's 19 Management aged 16 and, with a publishing deal with EMI, two years later she released her debut album *Frank* (2003) with Island Records.

MAJOR LABEL SUCCESS

Frank was well received by the critics, but the critical success of the album – with two BRIT Award nominations, a Mercury Music Prize nomination and an Ivor Novello Award, all in 2004 – was not matched by sales. Nevertheless, she performed at a number of festivals in 2004, including the Montreal International Jazz Festival.

It was at this time that she met her future husband, Blake Fielder-Civil. The end of the first phase of their relationship after a few months hit Winehouse hard, but she put her emotions to good use in her songwriting, and when *Back To Black* was released in 2006, the pain was apparent. The music had changed too, from the jazzy inflections of *Frank* to a soulful and catchy R&B sound. It was the best-selling album of 2007 in the UK, and was also a significant hit in the US.

ONLY THE
GOOD DIE YOUNG

If the break-up with Fielder-Civil had produced a great album, it also produced some erratic behaviour, fuelled by increasing drug and alcohol problems. The paparazzi smelt blood, and Winehouse began her uncomfortable reign as a tabloid queen. Her surprise reconciliation with Fielder-Civil in early 2007, followed by their impulsive marriage in May of that year, only made things worse, and Winehouse and her now-husband became heavy drug users.

BAD RELATIONSHIPS

The awards kept coming throughout 2007 and 2008, however, with Winehouse receiving a Brit Award in 2007 and five Grammys in 2008, the first British female artist to do so. The continuing success of *Back To Black* helped propel *Frank* back into the charts. But her live performances became increasingly erratic, and she often appeared drunk on stage.

Her relationship with Fielder-Civil ended in divorce in 2009, after which she spent some time in St Lucia, where she reportedly quit drugs, although her drinking increased. She began work on the follow-up to *Back To Black*, and in March 2011 recorded 'Body And Soul' with Tony Bennett. Nevertheless, a performance in Belgrade in June 2011 was so erratic that it led to the cancellation of the rest of the tour. When she died on 23 July 2011, the level of alcohol in her blood was five times the legal drink-drive limit.

DATE OF BIRTH

14 September 1983

DATE OF DEATH

23 July 2011

GENRES

Soul, R&B, pop

ACKNOWLEDGEMENTS

AUTHOR BIOGRAPHIES

Joel McIver (Foreword)

Joel McIver is the author of 20 books on music; another 30 exist in translation. His best-known book is 2004's *Justice For All: The Truth About Metallica*, which has sold close to 50,000 copies in several languages. He regularly appears on radio and TV and was labelled 'the top rock scribe writing today' in a 2009 anthology of music writing, but don't worry, he's really an OK guy.

Jason Draper (Author)

Jason Draper is the Reviews Editor of *Record Collector* magazine and author of the Flame Tree publications *Led Zeppelin Revealed* and *A Brief History Of Album Covers*. His Prince biography, *Prince: Chaos, Disorder & Revolution*, has been hailed as one of the 'best-written,

most-factual Prince biographies' available and translated into French and Danish editions. He lives in London with his wife and Jack Russell.

Jim Driscoll (Author)

Jim Driscoll is a freelance writer, editor and musician, and also works part-time as a composer's assistant. Having come of age in the 1980s, he prefers the music of almost any other era, with a particular penchant for the American folk tradition and 1960s psychedelic rock. His collections of banjos and vinyl LPs are both growing at an alarming rate, as are the discarded drafts of his first novel. He is the artistic director of the Ashley Wood Festival, a multi-arts festival near his adopted home town in Wiltshire.

PICTURE CREDITS

Corbis: Rafael Fuchs: 125. **Delta Haze Corporation**: 169. **Foundry Arts**: 171. **Getty Images**: AFP: 255; Archive Photos: 53, 181, 235, 275, 339; FilmMagic: 199, 297, 323; Getty Images Entertainment: 21, 25, 167, 229; Hulton Archive: 41, 83, 107, 131, 135, 149, 217, 317, 329; Michael Ochs Archives: 27, 29, 31, 37, 39, 47, 63, 65, 73, 79, 81, 87, 89, 91, 93, 95, 113, 115, 127, 157, 177, 193, 195, 201, 203, 219, 223, 231, 233, 237, 239, 243, 245, 247, 249, 259, 261, 267, 271, 273, 285, 299, 305, 313, 315, 335, 337, 341; Premium Archive: 103, 189, 251, 327; Redferns: 23, 33, 35, 45, 55, 57, 59, 61, 69, 71, 75, 77, 97, 99, 105, 109, 111, 119, 129, 137, 139, 141, 143, 145, 147, 161, 163, 165, 173, 175, 179, 183, 185, 187, 191, 205, 207, 213, 215, 225, 227, 241, 257, 263, 269, 277, 281, 289, 291, 301, 303, 307, 309, 311, 321, 331, 333; Time & Life Pictures: 287; WireImage: 123, 133, 197, 209, 253, 265, 293, 295. **Photoshot**: Picture Alliance: 221; Retna: 19, 49, 51, 67, 85, 101, 117, 151, 211, 279, 319, 345; Starstock: 121, 155; UPPA 159. **Press Association Images**: AP: 325; Paul Howell/AP: 283; Yui Mok/PA Archive: 343; Justin Thomas/EMPICS Entertainment: 153; Topham Picturepoint: 43.

FURTHER READING

Assante, E., *Legends of Rock: The Artists, Instruments, Myths and History of 50 Years of Youth Music*, White Star, 2007

Bene, D., *Randy Rhoads: A Life*, Roxx Productions, 2005

Billboard Guide to American Rock and Roll, Billboard Books, 1997

Bogdanov, V. (ed.), et al, *All Music Guide to Rock*, Backbeat, 2002

Bogdanov, V. (ed.), *All Music Guide to the Blues: The Definitive Guide to the Blues*, Backbeat, 2003

Christe, I., *The Sound of the Beast: The Complete Headbanging History of Heavy Metal*, William Morrow, 2003

Cochran, B. and Van Hecke, S., *Three Steps to Heaven: The Eddie Cochran Story*, Hal Leonard, 2003

Crawford, B. and Patoski, J., *Stevie Ray Vaughan: Caught in the Crossfire*, Little Brown & Company, 1994

Cross, C., *Heavier than Heaven: A Biography of Kurt Cobain*, Hyperion, 2002

Cross, C., *Room Full of Mirrors: A Biography of Jimi Hendrix*, Hyperion, 2005

Cutchin, R. (ed.), *The Illustrated Encyclopedia of Guitar Heroes*, Flame Tree Publishing, 2008

Cyr, M., *A Wished-for Song: A Portrait of Jeff Buckley*, Hal Leonard, 2002

Dann, T., *Darker than the Deepest Sea: The Search for Nick Drake*, De Capo Press, 2006

Draper, J., *Led Zeppelin Revealed*, Flame Tree Publishing, 2008

Draper, J., *The Rolling Stones Revealed*, Flame Tree Publishing, 2007

Du Noyer, P. (ed.), *The Illustrated Encyclopedia of Music*, Flame Tree Publishing, 2003

Ellinham, M., *The Rough Guide to Rock*, Rough Guides, 1996

Fielder, H., *The Beatles Revealed*, Flame Tree Publishing, 2010

Fong-Torres, B., *The Hits Just Keep On Coming: The History of Top 40 Radio*, Backbeat Books, 2001

George-Warren, H. et al, *The Rolling Stone Encyclopedia of Rock & Roll*, Fireside, 2001

Graff, G. and Durchholz, D., *MusicHound Rock: The Essential Album Guide*, Gale, 1998

Harrison, H., *Kurt Cobain, Beyond Nirvana: The Legacy of Kurt Cobain*, The Archives Press, 1994

Heatley, M. (ed.), *Rock & Pop: The Complete Story*, Flame Tree Publishing, 2006

Heatley, M. (ed.), *The Definitive Illustrated Encyclopedia of Rock*, Flame Tree Publishing, 2006

Hendrix, J. and McDermott, J., *Jimi Hendrix: An Illustrated Experience*, Atria Books, 2007

Ingham, C., *The Book Of Metal*, Carlton Books, 2002

Jeffries, N. (ed.), *The "Kerrang!" Direktory of Heavy Metal: The Indispensable Guide to Rock Warriors and Headbangin' Heroes*, Virgin Books, 1993

Kent, M., *The Who Revealed*, Flame Tree Publishing, 2010

Larkin, C., *Encyclopedia of Popular Music*, Virgin Publishing, 2002

Larkin, C., *The Virgin Encyclopedia of Heavy Rock*, Virgin Books, 1999

Larkin, C., *The Virgin Illustrated Encyclopedia of Rock*, Virgin Books, 1999

Logan, N. and Woffinden, B. (eds.), *The Illustrated New Musical Express Encyclopedia of Rock*, Hamlyn, 1976

Mandel, H. (ed.), *The Illustrated Encyclopedia of Jazz & Blues*, Flame Tree Publishing, 2005

McCulloch, B. and Pearson, B., *Robert Johnson: Lost and Found*, University of Illinois Press, 2003

McStravick, S. and Roos, J., (eds.), *Blues-rock Explosion: From The Allman Brothers To The Yardbirds*, Old Goat Publishing, 2002

Pascall, J., *The Golden Years of Rock & Roll*, Phoebus Publishing, 1974

Poe, R. and Gibbons, B., *Skydog: The Duane Allman Story*, Backbeat Books, 2006

Rolf, J. (ed.), *The Definitive Illustrated Encyclopaedia of Jazz and Blues*, Flame Tree Publishing, 2007

Shapiro, P., *The Rough Guide to Soul Music*, Rough Guides, 2000

Shirley, I., *Led Zeppelin Revealed*, Flame Tree Publishing, 2008

Smith, J., *Off the Record: An Oral History of Popular Music*, Warner Books, 1988

Spicer, A., *The Rough Guide to Rock (100 Essential CDs)*, Rough Guides, 1999

Strong, M.C., *The Great Rock Discography*, Canongate Publications, 2002

Thompson, D., *Pop*, Collectors Guide Publishing, 2000

Ward, G., *The Rough Guide To The Blues*, Rough Guides, 2000

Whitburn, J., *Billboard Top 1000 Singles 1955–2000*, Hal Leonard Publishing, 2001

INDEX

Page references in **bold** refer to the main entries, those in *italics* to illustrations. Hyphenated page references take no account of intervening illustrations.

351